OUT *of the* BOX
HOLIDAY BAKING

OUT *of the* BOX
HOLIDAY BAKING

Gingerbread Cupcakes, Peppermint Cheesecake, and More Festive Semi-Homemade Sweets

HAYLEY PARKER

The Countryman Press
A division of W. W. Norton & Company
Independent Publishers Since 1923

To my family—
the best taste-testers around

Copyright © 2018 by Hayley Parker

For information about permission to reproduce selections from this book, write to
Permissions, The Countryman Press, 500 Fifth Avenue, New York, NY 10110

For information about special discounts for bulk purchases, please contact
W. W. Norton Special Sales at specialsales@wwnorton.com or 800-233-4830

Manufacturing by LSC Communications, Crawfordsville
Production manager: Devon Zahn

Library of Congress Cataloging-in-Publication Data

Names: Parker, Hayley, author.
Title: Out of the box holiday baking : gingerbread cupcakes, peppermint
cheesecake, and more festive semi-homemade sweets / Hayley Parker.
Description: First edition. | New York, NY : The Countryman Press, a
division of W. W. Norton & Company, [2018] | Includes index.
Identifiers: LCCN 2018032594 | ISBN 9781682683255 (pbk.)
Subjects: LCSH: Baking. | Holiday cooking. | LCGFT: Cookbooks.
Classification: LCC TX765 .P29 2018 | DDC 641.81/5—dc23
LC record available at https://lccn.loc.gov/2018032594

The Countryman Press
www.countrymanpress.com

A division of W. W. Norton & Company, Inc.
500 Fifth Avenue, New York, NY 10110
www.wwnorton.com

10 9 8 7 6 5 4 3 2 1

CONTENTS

Introduction

The holidays are my favorite time of year, and I don't care who knows it! But chances are, if you're reading this book, you also have an affinity for the winter season . . . in which case, welcome! I am just crazy about the holidays for many reasons, including but not limited to: giving presents, Christmas shopping, holiday music, and of course, Christmas baking! I feel like the holiday season is basically an approved and sanctioned time to eat all the things, indulge constantly, and enjoy every minute of it. Or at least, it's *my* personal sanctioned time to indulge.

Since I've always enjoyed this time of year, I decided to write a book about it! *Out of the Box Holiday Baking* came to be because I always have such a hard time putting away my Christmas decorations and festive sprinkles. I tend to get moody when I can no longer hear Elvis's crooning voice singing my favorite Christmas tunes, and I really don't like whoever decided peppermint, gingerbread, and eggnog could *only* be seasonal flavors. I mean, why deprive yourself of the greatest holiday flavors just because it's June? Who says you shouldn't guzzle eggnog by the pool in the summertime? (Okay, I admit . . . that doesn't sound very pleasant. But that's the only exception!)

Christmas in the Parker household is notoriously insane. As kids, my parents would force us to stay in our rooms until six in the morning, when we could finally emerge—chaperoned—to our Christmas haul. But over the years and as we've grown older, you'd *think* we would have pushed the waking-up part back to a more conventional hour. Nope, no, nada. For many years, my siblings and I would convene in one of our bedrooms at one, two, three in the morning and whisper excitedly. We'd stare at the clock as it ticked by at a glacial pace, willing it to become six AM so we could open our loot. Eventually, my parents would hear us tinkering about and we'd all gather around the tree in the middle of the early morning to open presents. We'd open them all and then go nap within the piles of shredded wrapping paper until it was time to go to my Grammie Pat's house at nine AM.

Even though, as adults, my parents would say, "Don't get up early because the presents we got you aren't even that good," I was still so excited to wake up and spend time with my family. On Christmas Day after we opened our presents, I'd get in the kitchen and start baking cookies and candies for all of us to share. Christmas is just my all-time favorite holiday for that reason: sharing and spreading the joy!

When I started my blog, The *Domestic Rebel*, in January 2011, the holiday season had just passed, but I was also already planning what I was going to share on my blog for the following November and December. Not only do the holidays bring excellent traffic to my website, but I love that everyone is so eager to bake for friends and family—and that people discover my website and choose to make some of the recipes that I created in my little kitchen. It's humbling and truly flattering!

Since the holidays only happen once a year, *Out of the Box Holiday Baking* will act as your year-round resource for finding and creating the best holiday recipes. Of course, there's no hard and fast rule about when you should make each recipe—I'm always down for a peppermint cupcake in the spring or a gingerbread cookie in the summer—but I hope you'll enjoy flipping through the pages all year long! Whether you're an avid planner like I am and are seeking out the best recipes for your holiday cookie swap parties, or if you're just in the mood for some festive flavors, *Out of the Box Holiday Baking* will serve as your inspiration to baking up whimsical holiday desserts any time of year.

The aesthetic behind *Out of the Box Holiday Baking*—as well as my other two books, *Out of the Box Desserts* and *Two in One Desserts*—is simple: take everyday, ordinary ingredients like boxed cake mix and transform them into unique, extraordinary desserts! Of course, there are some scratch-made recipes in here, too, but I want baking to be FUN and exciting . . . not stuffy and full of rules. If you're wrinkling your nose at the idea of a cookbook calling for boxed cake, I guarantee you'll be converted with one bite!

One of the questions I get asked the most often is: "What do you do with all of your treats?" And the answer is, when I'm not scarfing them down at record speed, I enjoy giving them away to friends, family, neighbors, random strangers, ghosts, and really anyone willing to take a large quantity of desserts off of my hands. Of course, I try everything I make (quality control, obviously), but I can't eat everything I make because, frankly, they don't make pant sizes as large as I'd be. Also, I would love to be famous one day, but not for being the star of the newest reality show *Hayley: The Giant Dessert Lady*, in which a camera crew follows me as I waddle around eating cupcakes by the baker's dozen.

So how am I qualified to be writing my third cookbook, you ask? Despite my wildly popular website, I am a home cook just like you are. I am entirely self-taught because frankly, I didn't grow up with home-cooked meals. I was a self-proclaimed "drive-thru diva" who knew of all of the specials on all of the drive-thru menu boards. My parents loathed cooking, and I probably had microwave hot dogs for dinner three times a week. My chef skills came out of necessity, because yes, you can eat so many hot dogs in a week that you start to become a living, breathing hot dog yourself.

I turned on the Food Network and caught an episode of a famous thirty-minute meal show and raced to the store to buy the ingredients. I taught myself how to chop, dice, boil, and sauté and realized I truly loved cooking. I have always loved expressing myself, whether it be through my eclectic fashion choices or my crazy-colored rainbow hair, and cooking was just another way to express myself and share my love through food.

So whether you're a home cook like myself or an experienced pastry chef, I guarantee you'll find something you love in this book! From White Chocolate Peppermint Cupcakes (page 58) to Eggnog Cream Pie (page 112) and Chocolate-Covered Cherry Brownie Bites (page 95) to Red Velvet Whoopie Pies (page 43), there's truly something for every palate, age-group, and experience level. Everything's made simply and with love—which, frankly, is what the holidays are all about.

Enjoy, and Happy Baking!

XO, Hayley

Tips and Tricks

* To make cleanup a breeze, I line my pans with foil or parchment. To easily line a pan with foil, flip over the pan so it's upside-down. Take a piece of foil that's larger than the pan and gently wrap the foil around the bottom and sides of the pan, making the foil into the shape of the pan. Gently remove the foil and flip the pan, and then slide the shaped foil easily into the pan.

* To make cakes easier to remove from pans, line the springform or round cake pans with parchment rounds. Simply trace the pan's outline onto a piece of parchment paper and cut out the circle. Most stores sell parchment rounds, which are even easier as they already come in a 9-inch circle!

* Muffin liners are a must-use for cupcakes and muffins. The best part is, you can customize the cupcake with a fun printed liner!

* I recommend using softened butter for most of my recipes, unless otherwise specified. To soften butter, leave it at room temperature for about 30 minutes. Or in a pinch, microwave it unwrapped for 10 to 15 seconds.

* When measuring dry ingredients such as flour and cake mix, spoon the dry ingredients into a measuring cup and level off the top with a butter knife to ensure the most accurate measurement.

* If you're melting chocolate, such as chocolate chips or chocolate bars, make sure none of your tools—the bowl, spoons, spatulas, etc.—have water droplets inside or on them. Even the tiniest droplet of water can cause chocolate to seize and harden, rendering it absolutely useless.

Kitchen Must-Haves

* Cake mix—any and every flavor! I always have white, yellow, and chocolate on hand.

* Brownie mix—make sure it's a fudge brownie mix, which always yields the best results.

* Real butter—a must-have because it's the basis of so many recipes! And in most cases, there's no adequate substitution for it.

* Instant dry pudding mix—I always have vanilla and chocolate ready to go! Just make sure they're instant, as cook and serve will not work.

* Pie filling—an easy way to add fruit to a dessert! I like having cherry, apple, and berry available.

* Canola or vegetable oil

* Large eggs

* Pure vanilla extract

* All-purpose flour

* White sugar

* Brown sugar—dark or light! Dark will yield richer, more molasses-flavored results.

* Powdered sugar

* Baking soda

* Baking powder

* Cornstarch—my secret ingredient for fluffy cookies!

* Sprinkles, because you only live once!

* Heavy cream and milk

* Sweetened condensed milk

* Assorted baking chips—such as semisweet chocolate, vanilla, peanut butter, butter-scotch, and/or dark chocolate chips

* Aluminum foil and parchment paper

* Cooking spray

* A 9-by-13-inch rectangular baking pan, an 8-by-8-inch or 9-by-9-inch square baking pan, two round 9-inch cake pans, a 9-inch springform pan, a Bundt pan, a 12-cavity muffin tin, and baking sheets

* Silicone liners—they make baking cookies easy!

* A cookie dough scoop (I like the tablespoon-size one)

* An electric mixer (stand mixer or hand-held)

HANDY CONVERSIONS

1 cup	8 fl oz	16 Tbsps	48 tsps	237 ml
¾ cup	6 fl oz	12 Tbsps	36 tsps	177 ml
⅔ cup	5 fl oz	11 Tbsps	32 tsps	158 ml
½ cup	4 fl oz	8 Tbsps	24 tsps	118 ml
⅓ cup	3 fl oz	5 Tbsps	16 tsps	79 ml
¼ cup	2 oz	4 Tbsps	12 tsps	59 ml
⅛ cup	1 oz	2 Tbsps	6 tsps	30 ml

TO DOUBLE A RECIPE

1 cup	2 cups
½ cup	1 cup
⅓ cup	⅔ cup
¼ cup	½ cup
1 Tbsp	2 Tbsps
1 tsp	2 tsps
¾ tsp	1½ tsps
¼ tsp	½ tsps

TO CUT A RECIPE IN HALF

1 cup	½ cup
½ cup	¼ cup
⅓ cup	8 tsps
¼ cup	2 Tbsps
1 Tbsp	1½ tsps
1 tsp	½ tsp
¾ tsp	⅜ tsp
½ tsp	¼ tsp
¼ tsp	⅛ tsp

Cookie Tips and Tricks

* I always recommend baking your cookies on parchment paper or silicone liners. Nowadays, they have pre-cut parchment paper sheets made for cookie sheets, so they're easy and convenient!

* I could not live without my cookie dough scoops! For these recipes, I recommend a variety of sizes. The most standard size is a one-tablespoon-size scoop, but some cookies will require a two-tablespoon size. You can find these scoops at most stores including Walmart, Target, and stores like Crate and Barrel.

* For cut-out cookie recipes, keep in mind that the cookie yield will vary quite a bit based on the size of your cookie cutters. For instance, for my Perfect Cut-Out Sugar Cookies, I got 36 to 40 cookies out of them because I used smaller cutters (around 1 inch). However, for the Sugar Cookie Christmas Trees, which uses the same recipe, I got about 24 cookies because of the varying sizes of the cutters.

1

Crazy-Good Cookies

Nothing says the holidays quite like Christmas cookies, and I think Santa Claus himself would agree! In this chapter you'll find delightful cookie recipes suited for decorating, cookie trays, or late-night snacking!

Chocolate Caramel Thumbprint Cookies

The original idea for this recipe was going to be a dulce de leche thumbprint cookie . . . and that's what happened. But then I realized, sugar cookies + caramel + chocolate = Twix bars, and I knew I had to add chocolate. Then again, when has adding chocolate ever been a bad idea? Never, in the history of life. I love the combination of the sweet and tender sugar cookies with the milky, thick dulce de leche and the simple drizzle of semisweet chocolate. **24 COOKIES**

INGREDIENTS

One 18-ounce package sugar cookie mix
⅓ cup all-purpose flour
8 tablespoons (1 stick) butter, melted
1 large egg
One 13-ounce can dulce de leche
1 cup chocolate bark coating

NOTE: You may not use all of the dulce de leche for these cookies. Not sure what to do with the extra? Melt slightly and pour over ice cream sundaes, spread on top of brownies, or fill cupcakes!

1. Preheat the oven to 375°F. Line two baking sheets with parchment paper or silicone liners.

2. Combine the sugar cookie mix, flour, melted butter, and egg in a large bowl and stir until mixed together and a soft dough has formed. Using a tablespoon-size cookie dough scoop, drop the rounded dough balls 2 inches apart on the prepared baking sheets. Using your finger, make a depression in the center of the dough ball and fill with 2 teaspoons dulce de leche.

3. Bake for 10 to 12 minutes, rotating the pans halfway through the baking time, until the cookies are set and just barely golden brown. Cool on the baking sheets completely.

4. Melt the chocolate bark coating according to the package directions. Drizzle the melted chocolate evenly over the cookies. Allow the chocolate to set before serving.

Mexican Mocha Cookies

Full disclosure: I first made this recipe early on in my blogging career, and it probably hasn't seen the light of day since. That is a crime against humanity, because these cookies rock my socks off! I originally tasted a version of these at my friend Katie's Halloween party, but tweaked them to suit my tastes better. The addition of spicy cinnamon adds such a warm kick to the cookies, and the Kahlua helps, too!　**48 COOKIES**

INGREDIENTS

FOR THE COOKIES

16 tablespoons (2 sticks) butter, softened

1 cup granulated sugar

¾ cup brown sugar

2 large eggs

1 tablespoon vanilla extract

1 tablespoon instant espresso granules

1½ teaspoons ground cinnamon

1 teaspoon baking soda

½ teaspoon kosher salt

3½ cups all-purpose flour

1½ cups semisweet chocolate chips

FOR THE KAHLUA FROSTING

8 tablespoons (1 stick) butter, softened

6 tablespoons Kahlua

3 cups confectioners' sugar

Chocolate-covered espresso beans for garnish

1. Preheat the oven to 350°F. Line two baking sheets with parchment paper or silicone liners.

2. Cream 16 tablespoons butter, 1 cup granulated sugar, and ¾ cup brown sugar together in the bowl of a stand mixer until fluffy, 2 minutes. Gradually add in the eggs, one at a time, beating well after each addition, followed by the vanilla and espresso granules. Add in the cinnamon, baking soda, salt, and flour, and combine slowly until a soft dough is formed. Stir in the chocolate chips.

3. Using a tablespoon-size cookie dough scoop, drop rounded dough balls onto the prepared baking sheets 2 inches apart. Bake for 10 to 12 minutes, rotating pans halfway through the baking time, until the cookies are light golden brown and just about set on the top. Cool on the baking sheets completely.

4. For the frosting: Beat the remaining 8 tablespoons butter, Kahlua, and confectioners' sugar together in a medium bowl with an electric mixer until smooth and combined, 1 minute. Spread the frosting onto the cooled cookies and garnish with a chocolate-covered espresso bean.

Shortcut Gingerbread Men

So I should clarify that I am by no means a cookie artist. I am friends with cookie artists and they create these gorgeous masterpieces with some royal icing magic and a lot of patience, neither of which I possess. Let's just say my talents lie elsewhere, like being able to quote *The Simpsons* episodes or being a dog-whisperer. While my decorating skills are sub-par at best, I am a master at making the tastiest cookies, and really, that's what counts! You won't believe how easy these gingerbread people are to make! **20–24 COOKIES**

INGREDIENTS

1 small box instant butterscotch pudding mix

8 tablespoons (1 stick) butter, softened

½ cup brown sugar

1 large egg

1½ teaspoons ground cinnamon

2 teaspoons ground ginger

½ teaspoon ground cloves

½ teaspoon baking soda

¼ teaspoon kosher salt

1½ cups all-purpose flour

Royal icing, assorted candy, or sprinkle decorations for decoration, optional

1. Combine the dry pudding mix, butter, and brown sugar in the bowl of a stand mixer and cream until smooth, 2 minutes. Add in the egg until blended. Add in the cinnamon, ginger, cloves, baking soda, salt, and flour, and gently combine until a soft dough is formed. Cover and refrigerate the dough for 1 hour.

2. Preheat the oven to 350°F. Line two baking sheets with parchment paper or silicone liners.

3. Roll the cookie dough out until it is a quarter-inch thick on a lightly floured surface. Using cookie cutters, cut out gingerbread people shapes. Evenly place them on the prepared cookie sheets about 2 inches apart.

4. Bake for 10 to 14 minutes, rotating the pans halfway through the baking time, until golden brown. Cool on the baking sheets completely. Once cooled, decorate with royal icing, sprinkles, and assorted candies, if using.

Salted Nut Roll Blossoms

I know I'm not supposed to play favorites, but let's face it: sometimes your children make it pretty easy to choose. Don't blame me for stating the obvious! I tried to be unbiased about all of the treats for this book. I tried to love everything equally. But let me tell you—after making these exact cookies, I died and went to cookie heaven. There, I was able to see it clearly: these are my FAVORITE cookies in the book. I'm sorry, other recipes—you are beautiful and tasty in your own ways. But if you love peanut butter and need a fantastically soft, chewy, ultra-perfect cookie recipe, this is IT! **24 COOKIES**

INGREDIENTS

8 tablespoons (1 stick) butter, softened

¾ cup granulated sugar, plus ⅓ cup

½ cup brown sugar

¾ cup creamy peanut butter

1 large egg

1 teaspoon vanilla extract

1 teaspoon baking soda

½ teaspoon kosher salt

1½ cups all-purpose flour

4 salted nut roll candy bars, cut equally into 6 slices each (24 pieces total)

NOTE: Wondering what a salted nut roll candy bar is? These are a vintage classic: marshmallow surrounded by salty, crunchy peanuts! I love that the salted nut roll bites give these cookies a fluffernutter flavor. If you don't like marshmallow or cannot find the salted nut roll candy bars, feel free to use a Hershey's Kiss candy in the middle for a classic blossom cookie!

1. Preheat the oven to 350°F. Line two baking sheets with parchment paper or silicone liners.

2. Cream the butter, ¾ cup granulated sugar, and brown sugar together in the bowl of a stand mixer until fluffy, 2 minutes. Beat in the egg and vanilla until combined, followed by the baking soda, salt, and flour until a soft dough has formed.

3. Using a tablespoon-size cookie dough scoop, roll balls of cookie dough. Dredge the cookie dough balls into a bowl with the remaining ⅓ cup granulated sugar, coating all sides of the dough ball. Place the dough balls 2 inches apart on the prepared baking sheets.

4. Bake for 8 to 10 minutes, rotating the pans halfway through the baking time, until golden brown and set. Cool for 5 minutes on the baking sheets, then gently press a salted nut roll candy slice in the center of each cookie. Allow the cookies to continue to cool on the baking sheets or a wire rack.

Red Velvet Shortbread Cookies

I don't get invited to many parties, but when I do, I fret day and night about what I should bring. Should I make an old standby, or try something new and innovative? Believe me, it's a battle of heart and mind every single time. But one day while making this book, I decided to make these Red Velvet Shortbread Cookies—you know, to jazz things up a bit—and the result was marvelous! With a simple but elegant white chocolate drizzle, it immediately changed the game for my go-to party treat. **24 COOKIES**

INGREDIENTS

1¼ cups all-purpose flour

⅓ cup granulated sugar

2 tablespoons unsweetened cocoa powder

¼ teaspoon kosher salt

1 tablespoon red food coloring

8 tablespoons (1 stick) butter, cubed

1¼ cups white chocolate bark coating

1. Preheat the oven to 325°F. Line two baking sheets with parchment paper or silicone liners.

2. Combine the flour, sugar, cocoa powder, and salt in the bowl of a food processor. Pulse on low speed for 10 seconds so everything becomes combined. Add in the food coloring and cubed butter and pulse again until the mixture is crumbly. Pulse a few more times until the mixture forms itself into a ball.

3. Lightly flour a flat work surface. Roll out the cookie dough to a quarter-inch thickness. Using a 1-inch round cookie cutter, cut out circles of shortbread and place 2 inches apart on the prepared baking sheets.

4. Bake for 20 to 24 minutes or until the cookies are set and very lightly golden brown. Cool on the baking sheets completely. Once cooled, melt the white chocolate bark coating according to package directions. Drizzle the melted white chocolate evenly over the cookies. Allow the chocolate to harden and set before serving.

Old-Fashioned Oatmeal Cookies

So I know I said I don't play favorites with my desserts and then I lied and admitted I liked the Salted Nut Roll Blossoms the best. That's still true . . . but these Old-Fashioned Oatmeal Cookies are also tied for best in show. I am an oatmeal cookie purist—I don't like them with raisins OR chocolate chips because the oatmeal/brown sugar/slight cinnamon-spiced flavors need to be put on full display. With a light vanilla glaze, these cookies are seriously mind-blowing! **45 COOKIES**

INGREDIENTS

FOR THE COOKIES

2 cups old-fashioned oats

2 cups all-purpose flour

1 tablespoon baking powder

½ teaspoon baking soda

½ teaspoon kosher salt

2 teaspoons ground cinnamon

½ teaspoon ground nutmeg

16 tablespoons (2 sticks) butter, softened

1 cup brown sugar

½ cup granulated sugar

2 large eggs

1 teaspoon vanilla extract

FOR THE GLAZE

2 cups confectioners' sugar

5 tablespoons milk

½ teaspoon vanilla extract

1. Preheat the oven to 350°F. Line 2 baking sheets with parchment paper or silicone liners.

2. Pulse the oats a few times in a food processor using short bursts. You want the oats to have different textures—some oats will be completely intact, but others may be more finely ground. Pour the pulsed oats into a large bowl and add the flour, baking powder, baking soda, salt, and spices. Mix gently to combine.

3. Cream the butter, brown sugar, and granulated sugar together in the bowl of a stand mixer until fluffy, 2 minutes. Add in the eggs, one at a time, beating well after each addition, followed by 1 teaspoon vanilla extract. Gradually add in the oat mixture, beating well after each addition, until a soft dough is formed.

4. Using a tablespoon-size cookie dough scoop, drop rounded dough balls 2 inches apart on the prepared baking sheets. Bake for 10 to 12 minutes, rotating the pans halfway through the baking time, until the cookies are golden brown. Cool for 10 minutes on the baking sheets, then move the cookies carefully to wire racks to cool completely.

5. For the glaze: Whisk together the confectioners' sugar, milk, and ½ teaspoon vanilla extract until smooth and pourable. Gently spoon the glaze on each of the cookies and allow the glaze to set, 20 to 30 minutes, before serving.

Chai Snowballs

I was a precocious young girl when I first tried an iced chai tea latte. My dad used to take me to the bookstore every Friday night and we'd stop in the built-in café for a drink while we browsed books. I saw a really pretty stranger in line in front of me order a chai tea latte, and I figured if I ordered one, too, I'd inherit both her good looks and good taste. I took a sip and was very surprised at how good it was and how a gamble on a stranger's drink would forever change my café drink order. These snowballs are just like the original but with an aromatic warmth from chai spices. **25–30 COOKIES**

INGREDIENTS

16 tablespoons (2 sticks) butter, softened
¼ cup granulated sugar
2 tablespoons brown sugar
1 teaspoon vanilla extract
1 teaspoon ground cinnamon
1 teaspoon ground ginger
½ teaspoon ground cardamom
½ teaspoon ground nutmeg
⅛ teaspoon ground cloves
2 cups ground pecans
2 cups all-purpose flour
1 cup confectioners' sugar

1. Preheat the oven to 375°F. Line two baking sheets with parchment paper or silicone liners.

2. Cream the butter, granulated sugar, and brown sugar together in a large bowl with an electric mixer until fluffy, 2 minutes. Add in the vanilla and mix well. Add in the spices, ground pecans, and flour and beat on low speed until fully incorporated. The mixture will be crumbly but moist.

3. Using a tablespoon-size cookie dough scoop, drop rounded dough balls 1 inch apart on the prepared baking sheets. Bake for 10 to 14 minutes, rotating the pans halfway through the baking time, until the cookies are golden brown and set. Cool for 10 minutes, then carefully coat the cookies in some of the confectioners' sugar. Return the coated cookies to a wire rack to cool completely. Once cooled completely, coat the cookies in another layer of the confectioners' sugar.

Salted Caramel Macaroons

I am such a fan of coconut macaroons because they're like the easiest cookie out there. They don't need any special ingredients or tools, they don't need to chill, they don't need to rest, they don't need cucumber slices put over their eyes while you massage them and whisper that everything will be all right. They're just here to party and have a good time. While regular macaroons are a staple on your cookie tray, you should also make room for this salted caramel version. One ingredient swap makes these ultra decadent with buttery caramel flavor and a nice sprinkling of salt on top. It only looks and tastes fancy, I promise! **15–18 COOKIES**

INGREDIENTS
5½ cups shredded coconut
⅔ cup all-purpose flour
1 teaspoon vanilla extract
One 13-ounce can dulce de leche
Sea salt

1. Preheat the oven to 350°F. Line two baking sheets with parchment paper or silicone liners.

2. Toss together the shredded coconut and flour in a large bowl until the flour coats the coconut evenly. Add in the vanilla extract and dulce de leche and mix well—mixture will be very thick.

3. Using a tablespoon-size cookie dough scoop, drop rounded dough balls 1 inch apart on the prepared baking sheets. If any pieces of coconut are poking out of the dough ball, gently wet your fingers to press the coconut into the cookie. Sprinkle the tops of the cookies with sea salt.

4. Bake for 12 to 15 minutes, rotating the pans halfway through the baking time, until golden brown. Cool on the baking sheets completely before serving.

Perfect Cut-Out Sugar Cookies

So we've already established that I am no cookie-decorating aficionado, but that's okay! I have met many a decorated cookie that tasted . . . anticlimactic and sad. They looked gorgeous and mind-blowing but tasted stale and unappealing. Not these bad boys! The glaze may be simple, but the cookie is for sure the stand-out with its tender crumb, buttery vanilla flavor, and hint of lemon to perk them up. However, if you are feeling a touch feisty, add in a drop of almond extract and prepare to swoon at the flavor. **24–36 COOKIES**

INGREDIENTS

16 tablespoons (2 sticks) butter, softened

1½ cups confectioners' sugar

1 large egg

2 teaspoons vanilla extract

Zest of half a lemon

2 teaspoons baking powder

1 teaspoon kosher salt

3 cups all-purpose flour

Royal icing and assorted sprinkles for decoration, optional

NOTE: I love the way almond extract enhances the buttery richness of these cookies. However, my mom's allergic, so I often omit that when I'm serving them to her. If you can, I recommend using ½ teaspoon almond extract in place of the lemon zest for an added complex flavor.

1. Preheat the oven to 400°F. Line two baking sheets with parchment paper or silicone liners.

2. Cream the butter and confectioners' sugar together in the bowl of a stand mixer until fluffy, 3 minutes. Scrape down the sides of the bowl, then beat in the egg, vanilla extract, and lemon zest. Add in the baking powder, salt, and flour, and slowly beat on low speed until fully incorporated.

3. Lightly dust a flat work surface with flour and roll out the cookie dough until a quarter-inch thick. Using your favorite cookie cutters, cut out shapes and transfer to the prepared baking sheets, spacing them 2 inches apart.

4. Bake for 8 to 10 minutes until just barely browned—they shouldn't really have color at all. Cool completely on the baking sheets before decorating with royal icing and sprinkles, if using.

Sugar Cookie Christmas Trees

I think we can all agree that as kids, we'd decorate sugar cookies or build gingerbread houses during the holidays, but no one in my family moonlights as a chef. My parents or Grammie Pat would just buy us premade houses or cookies and give us a tub of frosting to work with. Fine by me! As a kiddo, I didn't care so much that it was premade; I just loved decorating something! These Sugar Cookie Christmas Trees are a modern-day approach to gingerbread house-building but are SO MUCH EASIER! **8 CHRISTMAS TREES (24 COOKIES)**

INGREDIENTS

1 batch Perfect Cut-Out Sugar Cookies (recipe on page 31)

12 tablespoons (1½ sticks) shortening

2 teaspoons vanilla extract

3½ cups confectioners' sugar

Green food coloring

Assorted sprinkles

NOTE: If you use different sized cookie cutters than I used, you may get more or less Christmas cookie trees than I did. Experiment with smaller sizes for smaller trees, or jumbo cutters for large trees!

1. Preheat the oven to 400°F. Line two baking sheets with parchment paper or silicone liners. Prepare one batch of the Perfect Cut-Out Sugar Cookie recipe.

2. Lightly flour a flat work surface. Roll out the sugar cookie dough to a quarter-inch thickness. Using three different size round cutters (I used ¾ inch, 1 inch, and 1½ inch), cut out circular shapes and place 2 inches apart on the prepared baking sheets.

3. Bake for 8 to 10 minutes or until set and barely golden brown—the cookies should still be very pale. Cool completely on the baking sheets.

4. Add the shortening and vanilla extract to the bowl of a stand mixer and beat until fluffy, 2 minutes. Gradually add the confectioners' sugar, beating well after each addition, until the frosting is light and fluffy. Beat in the green food coloring to your desired shade.

5. Fill a piping bag with the frosting and attach an open or closed-star tip of your choice. Place the largest cookie on a flat surface. Begin piping the frosting around the cookie clockwise until there is a circle of frosting. Sprinkle the perimeter of the frosted cookie with sprinkles of choice. Gently press the middle-size cookie on top and repeat with frosting and sprinkles. Lastly, gently press the smallest cookie size on top and repeat with frosting, but add a peak to represent the top of a Christmas tree. Decorate with sprinkles.

Polar Bear Cookies

People tell me all the time that I'm super creative . . . and beautiful, and intelligent, and amazing, and humble. KIDDING! But sometimes I feel pressure to do cutesy creative things. I can come up with some wacky-fabulous cupcake flavors, but turning a unicorn into a cake pop is so not my jam. So you can believe my excitement when I created these adorable and EASY Polar Bear Cookies! Kids and adults alike will have a blast creating the little bear faces, and I swear it could not be easier! I don't mean to humble-brag, but I may be a genius. (Kidding again. Sort of.) **20 COOKIES**

INGREDIENTS

One 16-ounce package white chocolate bark coating

20 vanilla sandwich cookies (such as golden Oreo)

60 white chocolate bark coating discs

40 eyeball sprinkles

20 black jelly beans

Edible bow adornments, optional

NOTE: You can make these into cookie pops by placing the still-wet cookie onto the top of a popsicle stick and allowing it to harden to the stick. Super cute for gift-giving!

1. Line a baking sheet with parchment paper or aluminum foil; set aside. Melt the white chocolate bark coating in a large bowl according to package directions, or until smooth and creamy.

2. Using a fork, dip each cookie one at a time into the white chocolate mixture, coating all sides of the cookie. Gently lift the cookie from the melted white chocolate and tap off any excess chocolate. Carefully place the coated cookie onto the prepared baking sheet. Working quickly, press two candy melt discs on either side of the top of the cookie for ears, then stick a candy melt disc on the lower half of the cookie for the snout. Place two eyeball sprinkles right above the candy melt disc for the eyes. If using the edible bow adornments, gently press one against the bottom of the cookie. Let the cookies set.

3. Dip the end of a toothpick into the remaining white chocolate and smear a little white chocolate on the back of a jelly bean. Press the jelly bean gently on the top of the "snout" for the nose. Allow the jelly beans to adhere before serving.

Snickerdoodle Spritz Cookies

Back to the part about my family not being chefs . . . they are most definitely not chefs. If we ever baked Christmas cookies, it came from a tube in the refrigerated section of the grocery store. So the idea of a spritz cookie—those adorable shaped sugar-like cookies made from a spritz press—was a faraway dream. I admit, I'd had spritz cookies before writing this book but I'd never made them until I started the process. Luckily, cookie presses aren't hard to find and they're very inexpensive! Plus, since these cookies are so petite, you can make quite a large batch from one basic dough recipe. Score! **70 COOKIES**

INGREDIENTS

16 tablespoons (2 sticks) butter, softened

1 cup confectioners' sugar

1 teaspoon vanilla extract

1 large egg

2 cups all-purpose flour

½ teaspoon kosher salt

⅓ cup granulated sugar

1 tablespoon ground cinnamon

NOTE: To ensure a successful spritz cookie, follow these tips. Hold the cookie press so that it is upright and the bottom is touching the baking sheet. Force the dough through the press until a cookie has been pushed out, then lift the press upward after the shape has been formed. If your dough is too soft and the cookie shapes aren't crisp, refrigerate the press briefly.

1. Preheat the oven to 375°F. Set out two nonstick baking sheets but do not grease them—the key to making spritz cookies is that they have to go on an ungreased baking sheet.

2. Cream the butter and confectioners' sugar together in the bowl of a stand mixer until fluffy, 2 minutes. Beat in the vanilla extract and the egg, mixing well. Add in the flour and salt and beat until a soft dough comes together.

3. Fill a cookie press with the cookie dough using your desired template. Press the cookie dough out onto the baking sheets a half-inch apart. Whisk together the granulated sugar and cinnamon in a small bowl and sprinkle the tops of the cookies with cinnamon sugar.

4. Bake for 6 to 8 minutes, rotating the pans halfway through the baking time, until the cookies are very light golden brown. Cool for 10 minutes on the baking sheets before transferring to a wire rack to finish cooling.

Chocolate Crinkles

There's a cookie bakery here in Sacramento that I happen to adore. They make the best soft and chewy cookies in a plethora of flavors. One of my favorites is their chocolate crackle cookie because it tastes like a cross between a fudgy brownie and a chewy cookie. It's a game-changer! When I experimented with this recipe, I realized these cookies tasted even BETTER than the original. They're so fudgy, gooey, soft, and chewy with that amazingly rich chocolate flavor and a light coating of sweet powdered sugar, you'll ask yourself, "What bakery?" **24 COOKIES**

INGREDIENTS

1 box chocolate fudge cake mix

8 tablespoons (1 stick) butter, melted

2 large eggs

1 teaspoon vanilla extract

¼ cup granulated sugar

⅓ cup confectioners' sugar

1. Preheat the oven to 350°F. Line two baking sheets with parchment paper or silicone liners.

2. Combine the cake mix, melted butter, eggs, and vanilla extract in a large bowl and stir until mixture is soft and combined. Using a tablespoon-size cookie dough scoop, drop rounded dough balls into a small bowl with the granulated sugar. Toss to coat, then place the sugared dough balls in a small bowl with the confectioners' sugar. Roll the dough balls so they're completely coated in the confectioners' sugar, then place them 2 inches apart on the prepared baking sheets.

3. Bake for 10 to 12 minutes, rotating the pans halfway through the baking time, until the edges are set. Cool the cookies completely on the baking sheets before serving.

Whipped Shortbread Cookies

What's the difference between whipped shortbread and regular shortbread? Once you try whipped shortbread, you'll never want to go back to boring, basic shortbread again! Seriously—whipping the ingredients together for a longer period develops a lovely, melt-in-your-mouth texture to the cookies and makes them very tender. Top them with sprinkles, candied cherries, or coarse sugar to send them really over the top! **36 COOKIES**

INGREDIENTS

24 tablespoons (3 sticks) butter, softened

¾ cup confectioners' sugar

2¼ cups all-purpose flour

¾ cup cornstarch

Candied cherries, sprinkles, or coarse sugar for topping

1. Preheat the oven to 300°F. Line two baking sheets with parchment paper or silicone liners.

2. Cream together the butter and confectioners' sugar in the bowl of a stand mixer, whipping on medium-high speed until fluffy, 3 minutes. Slowly add in the flour and cornstarch and continue beating until well blended.

3. Using a tablespoon-size cookie dough scoop, drop rounded dough balls 1 inch apart onto the prepared cookie sheets. Using your finger, make a small depression in the center of each cookie and place a candied cherry inside. If you're not using candied cherries, simply sprinkle some coarse sugar or sprinkles on the tops of the cookies.

4. Bake for 18 to 20 minutes, rotating the pans halfway through the baking time, until set and the bottoms are very light golden brown. Cool for 5 to 10 minutes on the sheets, then carefully transfer the cookies to wire racks to cool completely.

Red Velvet Whoopie Pies

When I made these whoopie pies, I had to get approval from my favorite Texans: my neighbors Ashley and Hayden. With one bite, Hayden exclaimed, "These are the BEST whoopie pies I've ever tried!" Needless to say, I was pretty flattered to hear that from a true Southerner who was well-versed in whoopie pies growing up. Try one for yourself and I think you'll agree! 8 WHOOPIE PIES

INGREDIENTS

FOR THE WHOOPIE PIES

1 box red velvet cake mix

½ cup vegetable or canola oil

2 large eggs

1 teaspoon vanilla extract

FOR THE FILLING

4 ounces cream cheese, at room temperature

4 tablespoons (½ stick) butter, softened

1 teaspoon vanilla extract

3 cups confectioners' sugar

1. Preheat the oven to 350°F. Line two baking sheets with parchment paper or silicone liners.

2. Combine the cake mix, oil, eggs, and 1 teaspoon vanilla extract in a large bowl and beat until smooth and blended. Drop heaping 2-tablespoon-size balls of dough 3 inches apart on the prepared baking sheets. If parts of the dough ball are sticking up and kind of spiky looking, lightly wet your finger to press the spikes down.

3. Bake for 12 to 15 minutes, rotating the pans halfway through the baking time, until the whoopie pies appear set. Cool completely on the baking sheets.

4. For the frosting: Whip the cream cheese, butter, and 1 teaspoon vanilla extract together in a large bowl with an electric mixer until smooth and fluffy, 2 minutes. Gradually add in the confectioners' sugar, beating well after each addition, until light and fluffy.

5. Pipe or spread the filling onto the flat bottom of a whoopie pie half. Gently press another whoopie cookie on top to make a sandwich.

Cakes and Cupcakes: Tips and Tricks

* I always recommend greasing your pans—even nonstick ones!—before adding in your cake batter. I like using the baking spray that has flour in it for easy release.

* Likewise, you can also line your cake pans with parchment rounds, which are available at most cake decorating and craft stores. This is such a lifesaver!

* The best method to ensure your cakes and cupcakes are finished baking? The toothpick test! A toothpick or cake tester inserted near the center of the cake or cupcake should come out clean or with moist but not wet crumbs.

* I find it is easiest to remove a Bundt cake from the pan when the pan and cake have cooled completely, unless otherwise specified.

2

Cakes and Cupcakes

Looking for a killer cake recipe to impress your guests for the holidays? Look no further than this chapter, packed with easy, impressive recipes that are sure to please everyone's palate!

Pumpkin Bundt Cake with Brown Butter Maple Icing

One of the most popular recipes on my blog during the holiday season has to be my pumpkin bread with brown butter maple icing. People go crazy for it because it's seriously the best pumpkin bread I've tried: moist, super pumpkin-y, and EASY! When I was brainstorming recipes for this book, I knew I had to transform that pumpkin bread into a pumpkin Bundt cake complete with the same irresistible icing as the recipe on my blog. You're welcome! **10–12 SLICES**

INGREDIENTS

FOR THE CAKE

1 box yellow cake mix

One 15-ounce can pumpkin puree

4 large eggs

½ cup vegetable or canola oil

½ cup brown sugar

2 tablespoons ground cinnamon

2 teaspoons ground ginger

1 teaspoon ground nutmeg

¼ teaspoon ground cloves

FOR THE ICING

8 tablespoons (1 stick) butter

¼ cup pure maple syrup

¼ cup milk

2½ cups confectioners' sugar

1. Preheat the oven to 350°F. Liberally grease a 10-cup Bundt pan with cooking spray—I like using the cooking spray with flour in it for easier release. Set aside.

2. Combine all of the cake ingredients into a large bowl and beat on low speed with an electric mixer until blended. Increase the speed to medium and beat well until fully combined and smooth. Pour the cake batter evenly into the prepared pan.

3. Bake for 40 to 45 minutes or until a toothpick inserted near the center comes out clean or with moist, not wet, crumbs. Cool in the pan completely.

4. While the cake bakes, make the icing: Melt the butter in a small saucepan over medium-low heat, stirring occasionally. Once the butter has melted, keep a close eye on it as it will brown quickly. Swirl the pan around as the butter pops, bubbles, and foams, until the butter turns a golden amber color and smells nutty and fragrant. Remove from the heat and cool completely.

5. Beat together the cooled browned butter, maple syrup, milk, and confectioners' sugar in a medium bowl with an electric mixer until smooth, 1 minute. Invert the cake onto a cake plate or stand. Drizzle the icing mixture evenly over the cake and let set for 10 minutes before serving.

Sticky Toffee Pudding Cake

Last Christmas, my family got my younger sister an ancestry DNA kit. We were 100 percent sure it would come back with a German heritage, but instead, it came back mostly British! Now we are all experiencing identity crises and questioning everything we've ever known. But in the midst of our existential crises, I realized—we have to make up for lost time by trying our native country's food, and that included sticky toffee pudding. Once I made this cake, we all came to terms that we're British now, and newly converted sticky toffee pudding lovers! **15–18 SLICES**

INGREDIENTS

2 cups chopped, pitted dates

2 teaspoons baking soda

8 tablespoons (1 stick) butter, softened

1⅔ cups granulated sugar

4 large eggs

1 tablespoon vanilla extract

3¼ cups all-purpose flour

2 teaspoons baking powder

½ teaspoon kosher salt

Vanilla ice cream and caramel sauce for serving

1. Combine the chopped dates and 2½ cups water together in a medium saucepan. Bring to a boil over medium-high heat, then remove from the heat and stir in the baking soda. Mixture may bubble as the baking soda is added. Cool to lukewarm.

2. Preheat the oven to 350°F. Liberally grease a 9-by-13 inch baking pan with cooking spray; set aside.

3. Cream the butter and granulated sugar together in the bowl of a stand mixer until fluffy, 2 minutes. Gradually add in the eggs, one at a time, beating well after each addition. Add in the vanilla extract, followed by the flour, baking powder, and salt. Turn the machine on low and slowly drizzle in the date mixture until fully combined and smooth.

4. Pour the batter evenly into the prepared baking pan and smooth out the top. Bake for 30 to 40 minutes or until a toothpick inserted near the center comes out clean or with moist, not wet, crumbs. Cool completely. Just before serving, top with a scoop of ice cream and drizzle liberally with caramel sauce.

Truffle Torte

If you're looking for a dessert to really impress your Christmas company, try my Truffle Torte! It tastes exactly like it came from a fancy-schmancy bakery or an elegant steakhouse because it's so rich and decadent with a complex chocolate flavor. Of course, it looks just as refined and elegant with a simple chocolate ganache topping, but my motto is: everything can be improved with some fun sprinkles! **10–12 SLICES**

INGREDIENTS

FOR THE CAKE

12 tablespoons (1½ sticks) butter, cubed

8 ounces semisweet chocolate, roughly chopped

6 large eggs

¾ cup granulated sugar

1 teaspoon vanilla extract

2 teaspoons instant espresso granules

½ teaspoon kosher salt

1 cup all-purpose flour

FOR THE GANACHE

1 cup bittersweet chocolate chips

½ cup heavy whipping cream

Fun sprinkles for garnish, optional

1. Preheat the oven to 350°F. Lightly grease the bottom of a 9-inch round springform pan. Place a parchment paper round in the bottom of the pan and spray the bottom and sides of the pan with more cooking spray; set aside.

2. Combine the cubed butter and chopped semisweet chocolate in a small bowl. Microwave the chocolate mixture for 30 seconds. Stir, then melt for another 30 seconds until completely smooth and melted. Cool for 5 minutes.

3. Whip the eggs and granulated sugar together in the bowl of a stand mixer on medium power for 5 minutes until the mixture has tripled in volume. Beat in the vanilla extract, then slowly and gradually stream in the melted chocolate. Add in the espresso granules, salt, and flour, and beat until the mixture comes together in a thick batter.

4. Pour the batter evenly into the prepared pan and smooth out the top. Bake for 30 to 40 minutes or until the top is set and crackled. After removing it from the oven, the top may sink into the cake some; this is normal, and remember, it'll be covered with ganache. Cool the cake completely.

5. For the ganache: Melt the chocolate chips and heavy whipping cream in a small bowl for 30 seconds in the microwave. Stir until melted. Pour the ganache mixture evenly over the truffle torte and smooth out the top. Top with sprinkles, if using. Refrigerate the cake for 2 hours or until set before serving.

Spiced Apple Cake

Most people think of pumpkin spice when fall approaches, but I happen to think of apple desserts first! One, because it's apple-picking season, and two, because admittedly I like apple desserts more than pumpkin (shh, don't tell!). This cake is moist and perfectly spiced with tender apple chunks swirled throughout. The glaze is a simple caramel drizzle that sends it over the top. For a real show-stopping cake, fill the center of the Bundt cake with miniature apples! **10–12 SLICES**

INGREDIENTS

FOR THE CAKE

1 box spice cake mix

½ cup brown sugar

1 cup buttermilk

½ cup vegetable or canola oil

3 large eggs

2 teaspoons vanilla extract

3 cups chopped, peeled, and cored apples

FOR THE CARAMEL GLAZE

¼ cup caramel sauce

2 tablespoons milk

3 cups confectioners' sugar

Miniature apples for garnish

1. Preheat the oven to 350°F. Liberally grease a 10-cup Bundt pan with cooking spray. Set aside.

2. Beat the cake mix, brown sugar, buttermilk, oil, eggs, and vanilla extract together in a large bowl with an electric mixer until smooth, 2 minutes. Fold in the chopped apples. Pour the batter evenly into the prepared pan and smooth out the top.

3. Bake for 40 to 50 minutes or until a toothpick inserted near the center comes out clean or with moist, not wet, crumbs. Cool completely in the pan.

4. For the caramel glaze: Whisk together the jarred caramel sauce, milk, and confectioners' sugar in a medium bowl until a glaze consistency has been achieved. Invert the Bundt cake onto a cake plate or stand. Drizzle the glaze evenly over the cake. If using, fill the center of the cake with miniature apples.

Gingerbread Cupcakes

I am such a goldilocks when it comes to ginger. Too much and it tastes like hand soap. Too little and it's bland. But if I get the nail on the head just right, it turns an ordinary spice cupcake into a seriously divine piece of heaven. I'm not sure why I initially thought to frost these perfect little cakes with marshmallow frosting, but the combination of sweet, fluffy vanilla bean marshmallow frosting and spicy, moist gingerbread cake is one for the books. This book, to be precise. **20–22 CUPCAKES**

INGREDIENTS

FOR THE CUPCAKES

1 box yellow cake mix

1 cup buttermilk

½ cup vegetable or canola oil

3 large eggs

¼ cup molasses

1 tablespoon ground ginger

2 teaspoons ground cinnamon

½ teaspoon ground nutmeg

¼ teaspoon ground cloves

FOR THE MARSHMALLOW FROSTING

8 tablespoons (1 stick) butter, softened

One 7-ounce jar marshmallow crème

2 teaspoons vanilla extract

1 tablespoon vanilla bean paste

3½ to 4 cups confectioners' sugar

¼ cup milk, as needed

Gingerbread men cookies for garnish

NOTE: Vanilla bean paste is a specialty ingredient found at craft and kitchen supply stores. I use both vanilla extract and vanilla bean paste because I want the flavor concentration from the extract but the gorgeous flecks of vanilla beans from the paste. If you cannot find the paste, simply use 3 teaspoons vanilla extract total.

1. Preheat the oven to 350°F. Line two muffin tins with 20 to 22 paper liners.

2. Combine the cake mix, buttermilk, oil, eggs, molasses, and spices in a large bowl and beat with an electric mixer until smooth, 2 minutes. Portion the batter evenly among the prepared muffin cups, filling each cup about three-quarters full.

3. Bake for 18 to 22 minutes or until a toothpick inserted near the center of the cupcake comes out clean or with moist, not wet, crumbs. Cool completely.

4. For the frosting: Cream the butter, marshmallow crème, vanilla extract, and vanilla bean paste together in the bowl of a stand mixer until fluffy, 1 minute. Gradually add in the confectioners' sugar, one cup at a time, until the frosting is light and fluffy, adding in the milk to thin out the frosting if it needs it. Note that you may not use all of the milk.

5. Pipe or spread the frosting onto the cooled cupcakes. Top each cupcake with a gingerbread man cookie.

Coconut Layer Cake

People ask me all the time, "How do you come up with your recipes?" The answer is, I freak people out at the grocery store. Seriously! For instance, for this recipe, I stood in the baking aisle and stared at a package of coconut in my hands as I telepathically willed a recipe to come to mind. The grocery store employees probably have me on a list in the back of crazy people to beware of. It usually takes 10 to 15 minutes of me standing there, non-verbally communicating with a package of candy before I come up with a recipe, so picture that as you will. However, I came up with this gem of a cake, so if loving coconut layer cake puts me on a crazy list, so be it! **10–12 SLICES**

INGREDIENTS

FOR THE CAKE

1 box white cake mix

1 cup buttermilk

½ cup vegetable or canola oil

3 large eggs

2 teaspoons coconut extract

1 small box instant coconut pudding mix

FOR THE FROSTING AND TOPPING

1 small box instant coconut pudding mix

⅓ cup confectioners' sugar

1 cup milk

4 ounces (½ package) cream cheese, at room temperature

One 8-ounce tub whipped topping, thawed

1½ cups shredded coconut

1. Preheat the oven to 350°F. Lightly grease the bottom of two 9-inch round cake pans. Place a parchment paper round in the bottom of each cake pan, then spray the bottom and sides of the pans again. Set aside.

2. Combine the cake mix, buttermilk, oil, eggs, coconut extract, and 1 box coconut pudding mix in a large bowl with an electric mixer. Beat until smooth and combined, 2 minutes. Pour the batter evenly among the two prepared pans.

3. Bake for 25 to 35 minutes or until a toothpick inserted near the center of each cake comes out clean or with moist, not wet, crumbs. Cool completely.

4. Meanwhile, for the frosting: In a large bowl, whisk together 1 box pudding mix, confectioners' sugar, and milk until combined and thickened, 2 minutes. Whisk in the cream cheese until fully incorporated. Fold in the whipped topping. Cover and refrigerate the frosting until thick and set, 1 hour.

5. Place one cake layer on a cake plate or stand. Top with half of the frosting, spreading the frosting out to the edges. Sprinkle the perimeter of the frosted cake with a half cup of the coconut. Top with the second cake layer and spread the remaining frosting over it. Then cover the top layer completely with shredded coconut. Cut into slices and serve!

White Chocolate Peppermint Cupcakes

INGREDIENTS

FOR THE CUPCAKES

1 box white cake mix

4 large egg whites

½ cup vegetable or canola oil

1 small box instant white chocolate pudding mix

FOR THE MOUSSE FILLING

½ cup peppermint baking chips (see Note on page 135)

1 cup plus ¼ cup heavy whipping cream

FOR THE WHITE CHOCOLATE FROSTING

16 tablespoons (2 sticks) butter, softened

1 cup white chocolate chips

¼ cup heavy whipping cream

1 teaspoon vanilla extract

⅓ cup milk

4 cups confectioners' sugar

Halved squares of peppermint bark for garnish, optional

1. Preheat the oven to 350°F. Line two muffin tins with 20 to 22 paper liners. Set aside.

2. Combine the cake mix, egg whites, oil, 1 cup water, and white chocolate pudding mix in a large bowl with an electric mixer, beating well until combined and smooth, 2 minutes. Portion the batter evenly among the prepared muffin cups, filling about three-quarters full.

3. Bake for 18 to 22 minutes or until a toothpick inserted near the center comes out clean or with moist, not wet, crumbs. Cool completely.

4. For the filling: Mix together the peppermint baking chips with ¼ cup heavy whipping cream in a small bowl. Microwave for 30 seconds, then stir until melted and smooth. Set aside. Meanwhile, whip the remaining 1 cup heavy whipping cream in the bowl of a stand mixer until stiff peaks form, 5 to 7 minutes. Whip in the melted peppermint chip mixture until fluffy and combined.

5. For the frosting: Cream the butter in the bowl of a stand mixer until fluffy, 2 minutes. While butter is creaming, microwave the white chocolate chips with ¼ cup heavy whipping cream in a small bowl for 30 seconds, stirring until melted. Stream in the melted white chocolate to the butter mixture, followed by the vanilla extract and milk. Gradually add in the confectioners' sugar, beating well after each addition, until the mixture is light and fluffy.

6. To assemble: Core the cupcakes with a cupcake corer or pairing knife, discarding the centers. Pipe the mousse filling into the center of each cored cupcake. Pipe or spread the white chocolate frosting evenly over each cupcake, taking care to cover the mousse filling with the frosting. Top each frosted cupcake with a halved peppermint bark square, if using.

Every couple of years, my family and I would drive two hours down to San Francisco during the holidays. We'd walk around our usual spots: Fort Mason, Fisherman's Wharf for clam chowder, the Ferry Building, and of course, Ghirardelli's factory. If you've been there, you know you can smell the intoxicating aroma as chocolate wafts into the sea-salted air. We'd order our usual sundaes in their ice cream parlor and I'd always grab a bag of peppermint bark to go. Theirs is my all-time favorite, and it was the inspiration for these cupcakes! **20–22 CUPCAKES**

Fruitcake Cupcakes

I know fruitcake gets a lot of flak, but I knew if I wrote a holiday-themed cookbook without a single fruitcake recipe, someone somewhere would be offended. Not to mention, I aim to please and took it as a personal challenge to make the most delicious fruitcake recipe I could think of: cupcakes! I think the problem people have with fruitcake is that it's usually stale and dry, which is basically the number-one offense for a cake. My cupcakes, however, are moist, soft, and brimming with fresh flavor. Never again will fruitcake be the ugly duckling of desserts! **18–20 CUPCAKES**

INGREDIENTS

FOR THE CAKE

1 box spice cake mix

1 cup orange juice

½ cup vegetable or canola oil

3 large eggs

Zest of one orange

1 teaspoon ground ginger

1½ cups fruitcake mix (See Note)

FOR THE FROSTING

16 tablespoons (2 sticks) butter, softened

1 teaspoon vanilla extract

Juice of one orange

3½ cups confectioners' sugar

¼ cup milk

Candied cherries for garnish

NOTE: Fruitcake mix can usually be found in the baking aisle at most grocery stores, or in the holiday aisle during the holiday season. It consists of chopped-up candied fruit like pineapple, orange rind, and cherries. Make sure your fruit cake mix is finely chopped so it disperses around the cupcakes evenly.

1. Preheat the oven to 350°F. Line two muffin tins with 18 to 20 paper liners; set aside.

2. Combine the cake mix, 1 cup orange juice, oil, eggs, orange zest, and ground ginger in a large bowl with an electric mixer and beat until smooth, 2 minutes. Fold in the fruitcake mix. Portion the batter evenly among the prepared muffin cups, filling about three-quarters full.

3. Bake for 18 to 22 minutes or until a toothpick inserted near the center comes out clean or with moist, not wet, crumbs. Cool completely.

4. For the frosting: Cream the butter, vanilla extract, and juice of one orange together in the bowl of a stand mixer until fluffy, 1 minute. Gradually add in the confectioners' sugar, beating well after each addition, alternating adding in the milk until the frosting is light and fluffy.

5. Pipe or spread the frosting onto the cooled cupcakes, then top with a candied cherry before serving.

Cranberry Orange Crumb Cake

INGREDIENTS

FOR THE CAKE

12 tablespoons (1½ sticks) butter, softened

1 cup granulated sugar

2 large eggs

1 tablespoon vanilla extract

Zest and juice from one medium orange

1 cup sour cream

2 cups all-purpose flour

1¼ teaspoons baking powder

½ teaspoon baking soda

½ teaspoon kosher salt

2 cups fresh or frozen cranberries

FOR THE CRUMB AND GLAZE

1 cup brown sugar

1¼ cups all-purpose flour

1 teaspoon ground cinnamon

8 tablespoons (1 stick) butter, melted

1 cup chopped walnuts

2 cups confectioners' sugar

⅓ cup orange juice

NOTE: If you cannot find fresh cranberries, many grocery stores carry frozen cranberries in the frozen fruit section. Just toss the frozen cranberries into the cake batter recipe without thawing. However, if you cannot find fresh OR frozen cranberries, you can substitute dried cranberries, but note that the cranberry flavor may not be as prominent as if it would be when you use fresh.

1. Preheat the oven to 350°F. Lightly grease a 9-inch round springform pan with cooking spray. Place a parchment paper round in the bottom of the pan, then spray the bottom and sides of the pan again. Set aside.

2. Cream 12 tablespoons butter and granulated sugar together in the bowl of a stand mixer until fluffy, 2 minutes. Add in the eggs, one at a time, beating well after each addition, followed by the vanilla extract, orange zest, and juice from one orange. Beat in the sour cream, followed by the flour, baking powder, baking soda, and salt until a thick, smooth batter forms. Fold in the cranberries. Spread the cake into the prepared pan evenly.

3. For the crumb: Combine the brown sugar, flour, cinnamon, and 8 tablespoons melted butter and stir until moistened. Fold in the chopped walnuts. Crumble the crumb mixture evenly over the cake. It will seem like a lot of crumb, but this is okay—you want to lay it on thick!

4. Bake the cake for 60 to 75 minutes or until a toothpick inserted near the center comes out clean or with moist, not wet, crumbs. Cool completely, noting that the cake may sink slightly in the middle. This is normal.

5. For the glaze: Mix the confectioners' sugar and orange juice until smooth. Drizzle evenly over the crumb topping before serving.

One of the more popular recipes on my blog is a cranberry walnut crumb cake, and for good reason: It's great for breakfast, brunch, or dessert; it's packed with fresh cranberry flavor; and it just feels like a giant, cozy hug. However, for this book I jazzed up my original recipe with lots of fresh orange zest and a zippy orange glaze that really elevates the brightness of the tart cranberries. I think you'll agree! **10–12 SLICES**

Eggnog Bundt Cake

You know the famous Bundt cake bakery, right? Well, I had never tried them before because Bundts sometimes have a tendency to be dry. One day, I got a coupon in the mail to try one of their baby cakes for free, so I took advantage. Hello, free cake is free cake, people! I thought it was really good . . . until I made this Bundt cake! With its rich eggnog flavor and moist crumb, it is spectacular . . . and totally needs its own bakery named after it. **10–12 SLICES**

INGREDIENTS

FOR THE CAKE

1 box vanilla cake mix

1 cup eggnog

½ cup vegetable or canola oil

3 large eggs

1 small box instant vanilla pudding mix

1 teaspoon rum extract

1 teaspoon ground nutmeg

1 teaspoon ground cinnamon

FOR THE FROSTING

4 ounces (½ package) cream cheese, at room temperature

2 tablespoons eggnog

1 teaspoon vanilla extract

2 cups confectioners' sugar

Holiday sprinkles for garnish, optional

1. Preheat the oven to 350°F. Liberally grease a 10-cup Bundt pan with cooking spray; set aside.

2. Combine the cake mix, 1 cup eggnog, oil, eggs, vanilla pudding mix, rum extract, and spices in a large bowl with an electric mixer, creaming together until smooth, 2 minutes. Pour the batter evenly into the prepared pan and smooth out the top.

3. Bake for 40 to 45 minutes or until a toothpick inserted near the center comes out clean or with moist, not wet, crumbs. Cool completely in the pan before gently inverting the cake onto a cake plate or stand.

4. For the frosting: Whisk together the cream cheese, 2 tablespoons eggnog, vanilla extract and confectioners' sugar together in a medium bowl until fluffy and smooth, 1 minute. Drizzle the glaze evenly over the cake. If using holiday sprinkles, top the glaze with the sprinkles. Allow the glaze to set briefly before serving, 10 minutes.

Red-Hot Cinnamon Cupcakes

I know you're probably wondering how hot cinnamon candies are reminiscent of Christmas . . . and the answer is because truthfully, hot cinnamon bears are one of my dad's favorite candies. When I was older and jaded about Santa Claus (as teenagers are, among other things), I'd help my mom shop for stocking stuffers the day before Christmas Eve. We'd always hunt down a bag of cinnamon bears for my dad's stocking. He always delighted in those spicy gummy bears, so they served as an inspiration for these punchy cinnamon cupcakes! **20–22 CUPCAKES**

INGREDIENTS

FOR THE CAKE

1 box white cake mix

½ cup vegetable or canola oil

3 large eggs

2 teaspoons cinnamon extract

1 cup red hot cinnamon candies, coarsely crushed

FOR THE FROSTING AND TOPPING

16 tablespoons (2 sticks) butter, softened

1 teaspoon vanilla extract

½ teaspoon cinnamon extract

¼ cup heavy whipping cream

3 cups confectioners' sugar

½ cup red hot cinnamon candies, finely crushed

Cinnamon bears for garnish

1. Preheat the oven to 350°F. Line two muffin tins with 20 to 22 paper liners; set aside.

2. Combine the cake mix, 1 cup water, oil, eggs, and cinnamon extract in a large bowl with an electric mixer until smooth, 2 minutes. Fold in 1 cup crushed red hot cinnamon candies. Portion the batter evenly among the prepared muffin cups, filling about three-quarters full.

3. Bake for 18 to 22 minutes or until a toothpick inserted near the center comes out clean or with moist, not wet, crumbs. Cool completely.

4. For the frosting: Cream together the butter, 1 teaspoon vanilla extract, and ½ teaspoon cinnamon extract until fluffy, 1 minute. Alternate adding the heavy whipping cream and the confectioners' sugar, beating well after each addition until frosting is light and fluffy. Stir in ½ cup crushed red hot cinnamon candies.

5. Pipe or spread the frosting onto the cooled cupcakes. Top with a cinnamon bear gummy candy.

Pecan Pie Cupcakes

Pie is one of my all-time favorite desserts; I've never tried a pie I didn't like. For the longest time, I had some mysterious grudge against pecan pie, which is as insane as it sounds. I swore I wouldn't like it, but like my phases with turquoise eye-shadow and Swedish pop bands, I eventually got over it and embraced the love of pecan pie. These cupcakes have a decadent pecan pie filling that is probably going to be illegal in all fifty states when word gets out. Don't say I didn't warn you! **22–24 CUPCAKES**

INGREDIENTS

FOR THE PECAN PIE FILLING

1½ cups chopped pecans

1 cup granulated sugar

⅔ cup dark corn syrup

5½ tablespoons melted butter

2 large eggs

1 tablespoon vanilla extract

FOR THE CUPCAKES

1 box white cake mix

1 cup dark brown sugar

1 cup buttermilk

½ cup vegetable or canola oil

3 large eggs

1 teaspoon vanilla extract

FOR THE FROSTING

16 tablespoons (2 sticks) butter, softened

¼ cup brown sugar

1 teaspoon vanilla extract

3 cups confectioners' sugar

¼ cup heavy whipping cream

Pecan halves for garnish

1. Make your filling first, as it needs time to cool and set. Combine the pecans, granulated sugar, dark corn syrup, 5½ tablespoons melted butter, 2 eggs, and 1 tablespoon vanilla extract in a medium saucepan over medium-high heat. Bring to a boil, stirring frequently, then reduce the heat to medium-low and simmer until thickened, 6 to 8 minutes. Remove from the heat and let cool completely or to room temperature.

2. Preheat the oven to 350°F. Line two muffin tins with 22 to 24 paper liners; set aside. Combine the cake mix, 1 cup dark brown sugar, buttermilk, oil, 3 eggs, and 1 teaspoon vanilla extract in a large bowl with an electric mixer until smooth, 2 minutes. Portion the batter evenly among the prepared muffin tins, filling about three-quarters full.

3. Bake the cupcakes for 18 to 22 minutes or until a toothpick inserted near the center comes out clean or with moist, not wet, crumbs. Cool completely, then use a cupcake corer or paring knife to core the center of the cupcake. Spoon a heaping tablespoon of pecan pie filling into each cupcake center, filling all the way to the top of the cupcake.

4. For the frosting: Cream together 16 tablespoons butter, ¼ cup brown sugar, and vanilla extract in the bowl of a stand mixer until fluffy, 2 minutes. Gradually add in the confectioners' sugar, beating well after each addition while alternating with the heavy whipping cream until the frosting is light and fluffy. Pipe or spread the frosting onto each cooled cupcake. Top with a pecan half.

Sweet Potato Sheet Cake

For many years, we'd go down to my Grammie Pat's house for Thanksgiving dinner, and every year, she'd make a huge batch of sweet potatoes. Besides her and my uncle, no one ever ate them. I wondered if maybe she thought, "All right, this year is the year someone tries the sweet potatoes!" Well, apparently it worked on me, because I tried a spoonful and was hooked. You just can't say no to the sweet gooiness of the soft, whipped potatoes and the tantalizing, bubbly marshmallow topping. This cake is an homage to that first fateful bite I took, and is a reminder that sweet potatoes and marshmallows should always be BFFs. **15–18 SLICES**

INGREDIENTS

FOR THE CAKE

One 15-ounce can sweet potato puree

1½ cups granulated sugar

1 cup vegetable or canola oil

2 teaspoons vanilla extract

4 large eggs

2 cups all-purpose flour

2 teaspoons baking powder

1 teaspoon baking soda

2 teaspoons ground cinnamon

½ teaspoon ground nutmeg

½ teaspoon ground ginger

½ teaspoon kosher salt

FOR THE MARSHMALLOW FROSTING

8 tablespoons (1 stick) butter, softened

One 7-ounce jar marshmallow crème

1 teaspoon vanilla extract

3 cups confectioners' sugar

¼ cup heavy whipping cream

Assorted sprinkles for garnish, optional

1. Preheat the oven to 350°F. Liberally grease a 9-by-13 inch baking pan with cooking spray; set aside.

2. Mix the sweet potato puree and granulated sugar in the bowl of a stand mixer until combined. Carefully stream in the oil and 2 teaspoons vanilla extract, beating on low speed, followed by the eggs, one at a time. Add in the flour, baking powder, baking soda, spices, and salt, and mix until smooth. Pour the batter evenly into the prepared pan and smooth out the top.

3. Bake for 25 to 30 minutes or until a toothpick inserted near the center comes out clean or with moist, not wet, crumbs. Cool completely.

4. For the frosting: Beat the butter, marshmallow crème, and 1 teaspoon vanilla extract together in the bowl of a stand mixer until creamy, 2 minutes. Gradually add in the confectioners' sugar, beating well after each addition, and streaming in the heavy whipping cream to thin it out if necessary. Mix until the frosting is light and fluffy.

5. Spread the frosting evenly over the cake and top with sprinkles, if using.

Mimosa Cupcakes

Christmas morning in the Parker household is a crazy time. First, our family of five wakes up at the crack of dawn to open presents. After our house adequately looks like a tornado ripped through it with mountains of torn wrapping paper everywhere, I sneak into the kitchen to whip up a quick breakfast and some mimosas for my mom and I. We cheers with our bubbly glasses of heaven and it's a small gesture that totally kicks off the rest of the wonderful holiday. I knew I had to create something reminiscent of our mimosas, and these cupcakes are it! **20–22 CUPCAKES**

INGREDIENTS

FOR THE CUPCAKES

1 box white cake mix

¾ cup champagne

½ cup buttermilk

⅓ cup vegetable or canola oil

3 large egg whites

Zest of one orange

FOR THE FROSTING

12 tablespoons (1½ sticks) butter, softened

½ teaspoon vanilla extract

¼ cup champagne

3 tablespoons orange juice

4 cups confectioners' sugar

Sprinkles and clementine wedges for garnish, optional

NOTE: When cooking with champagne, you don't need to use a pricey version! However, I *do* recommend you use champagne you would also like to drink. A good rule of thumb: when working with wine in recipes, be it sweet or savory—choose one you'd also enjoy on the side. If you wouldn't drink it, don't cook with it!

1. Preheat the oven to 350°F. Line two muffin tins with 20 to 22 paper liners; set aside.

2. Combine the cake mix, ¾ cup champagne, buttermilk, oil, egg whites, and orange zest in a large bowl with an electric mixer and mix until smooth, 2 minutes. Portion the batter evenly among the prepared muffin cups, filling about three-quarters full.

3. Bake for 18 to 22 minutes or until a toothpick inserted near the center comes out clean or with moist, not wet, crumbs. Cool completely.

4. For the frosting: Cream together the butter and vanilla extract until smooth, 1 minute. Add in ¼ cup champagne and orange juice and mix slowly. Gradually add in the confectioners' sugar, beating well after each addition until the frosting is light and fluffy.

5. Pipe or spread the frosting onto the cooled cupcakes. Top with sprinkles and a clementine segment, if using.

Black Forest Cupcakes

I'm not the biggest fan of change, so it took me a long time before I tried a black forest cake. What can I say? I'm a girl who appreciates routine and enjoys what I know I already like. But then again, what's not to like about black forest cake? Chocolate, cherry, a hint of almond . . . all good things wrapped up in one pretty package. And once I hopped on that black forest train, you can bet it was hard for me to come off! Thankfully I don't have to, because I have these mouthwatering cupcakes to keep me satisfied! **20–22 CUPCAKES**

INGREDIENTS

FOR THE CUPCAKES

1 box chocolate cake mix

1 cup buttermilk

½ cup vegetable or canola oil

3 large eggs

One 21-ounce can cherry pie filling

FOR THE FROSTING

16 tablespoons (2 sticks) butter, softened

1 teaspoon vanilla extract

1 teaspoon almond extract

3½ cups confectioners' sugar

¼ cup heavy whipping cream

NOTE: Not sure what to do with your leftover cherry pie filling? Add it into a milkshake; spoon it over ice cream, yogurt, or pudding; or pour the rest of it into a miniature graham cracker crust and top with whipped cream for a mini pie!

1. Preheat the oven to 350°F. Line two muffin tins with 20 to 22 paper liners; set aside.

2. Combine the cake mix, buttermilk, oil, and eggs in a large bowl with an electric mixer and mix until smooth, 2 minutes. Portion the batter evenly among the prepared muffin cups, filling about three-quarters full.

3. Bake for 18 to 22 minutes or until a toothpick inserted near the center comes out clean or with moist, not wet, crumbs. Cool completely, then use a cupcake corer or a paring knife to remove the core of each cupcake. Discard the insides. Fill the insides of the cupcakes with some of the cherry pie filling.

4. For the frosting: Cream together the butter, vanilla extract, and almond extract until smooth and fluffy, 2 minutes. Gradually add in the confectioners' sugar, one cup at a time, alternating adding in the heavy whipping cream until the frosting is light and fluffy.

5. Pipe or spread the frosting onto the cooled cupcakes, taking care to cover the hole in the middle of each cupcake. Spoon cherry pie filling evenly over the tops of the cupcakes, and note that you may not use all of the cherry pie filling (see Note).

Some Tips for Bar Recipes

* To easily line your pans with foil or parchment, flip the pan upside down and pull out a piece of foil or parchment that's larger than the pan's bottom. Gently press the foil or parchment around the edges of the pan to create a pan shape within the foil. Remove the foil, flip over the pan, and place the perfectly measured foil into the pan!

* I always grease my foil and parchment just to be safe. Nonstick cooking spray, butter, or shortening will work!

* To ensure everything is evenly cooked, I use a toothpick or cake tester to test the doneness in the center of the bar recipes. A toothpick that comes out clean or with moist—not wet!—crumbs is usually good to go.

3

Blondies, Brownies, and Bars

Whether you prefer fudgy brownies or brown sugary blondies, there's truly something for everyone in this fantastic chapter!

Cranberry Crumble Bars

I think most people forget about cranberries after November. We generally only consider cranberry sauce for the Thanksgiving dinner, and then we all move on with our lives, leaving those cranberry bogs in the dust. What did cranberries ever do to you, huh? I happen to love cranberry sauce on my sandwiches, but I never really thought about it for my desserts . . . until now. These crumble bars have a cranberry punch that's irresistible—tart, sweet, and zesty from a touch of orange. You don't want to skip over this recipe! **15–18 BARS**

INGREDIENTS

1 box yellow cake mix

12 tablespoons (1½ sticks) butter, softened

1 large egg

½ cup brown sugar

2 cups quick-cooking oats

One 14-ounce can whole berry cranberry sauce

Zest of half an orange

1 cup fresh or frozen cranberries, halved

1. Preheat the oven to 350°F. Line a 9-by-13 inch baking pan with foil or parchment, extending the sides of the foil over the edges of the pan. Spray the foil lightly with cooking spray.

2. Mix the yellow cake mix, softened butter, egg, and brown sugar in a medium bowl until just about combined. Stir in the oats as best as you can (however, it is easier to use your hands to get everything fully incorporated). Reserve 1½ cups of this dry mixture.

3. Spread the remaining mixture into the bottom of the prepared pan. Use your hands to gently press the crust mixture evenly into the bottom of the pan. Bake for 15 minutes, then remove from the oven but keep the oven on.

4. Fold the orange zest into the whole berry cranberry sauce. Spread the cranberry sauce evenly over the crust carefully. Top with the halved fresh cranberries, followed by the remaining crumb mixture. Bake for an additional 20 to 25 minutes or until the top is golden brown and the filling is bubbly.

5. Cool completely before cutting into squares.

Pomegranate Raspberry Bars

Long ago, in a galaxy down the street, I worked at a frozen yogurt shop. It was an awesome job because I got free yogurt every day, and for two years, I actually can confidently say I did eat yogurt every single day. While my order changed with the flavors, whenever we had pomegranate raspberry sorbet, I always looked forward to it. It was sweet and refreshing with a cool, tart bite and it was the inspiration for these gooey, zippy bars! **15–18 BARS**

INGREDIENTS

FOR THE CRUST

1 box white cake mix

8 tablespoons (1 stick) butter, melted

1 large egg

FOR THE FILLING AND TOPPING

One 8-ounce package cream cheese, at room temperature

3 large eggs

One 16-ounce box confectioners' sugar

One 1.25-ounce package freeze-dried raspberries, finely ground into powder

1 ounce raspberry gelatin powder

4 tablespoons butter, melted

¼ cup pomegranate juice

Additional confectioners' sugar, fresh pomegranate arils, and raspberries for garnish

1. Preheat the oven to 350°F. Line a 9-by-13 inch baking pan with foil or parchment paper, extending the foil over the edges of the pan. Spray the foil lightly with cooking spray; set aside.

2. Combine the crust ingredients in a large bowl and stir until moistened and incorporated. Press the crust mixture evenly into the bottom of the prepared pan.

3. For the filling: Beat the cream cheese in the bowl of a stand mixer until fluffy, 1 minute. Gradually add in the eggs, one at a time, beating well after each addition. Beat in the confectioners' sugar, followed by the freeze-dried raspberry powder and raspberry gelatin powder. Lastly, add in the ¼ cup melted butter and pomegranate juice and mix slowly to combine, scraping the sides of the bowl so everything is completely combined.

4. Pour the mixture evenly over the crust layer and smooth out the top. Bake for 38 to 45 minutes or until the top is light golden brown and the center is just about set. If it jiggles slightly, that's okay—but it should mostly be set. Cool completely at room temperature, then refrigerate at least 2 hours before cutting into squares.

5. Just before serving, sprinkle the tops of the bars with the additional confectioners' sugar, pomegranate arils, and fresh raspberries.

Christmas Blondies

These blondies were *this close* to being named Hayley's Blondies because truthfully, they have everything I love in a blondie: cranberries, pistachios, and so much white chocolate it'd make Santa Claus blush. What I love about these buttery blondies is the flavors all play off of each other so well, and because they're festively colored, too, with red, white, and green colors swirled throughout. If you're looking for a blondie recipe that screams Christmastime, these are for you! **15–18 BLONDIES**

INGREDIENTS

16 tablespoons (2 sticks) unsalted butter

2 cups brown sugar

2 large eggs

1 tablespoon vanilla extract

1 teaspoon baking soda

½ teaspoon kosher salt

2 cups all-purpose flour

½ cup dried cranberries

½ cup shelled pistachios

1 cup white chocolate chips, divided

1. Preheat the oven to 350°F. Line a 9-by-13 inch pan with foil or parchment paper, extending the sides of the foil over the edges of the pan. Spray the foil lightly with cooking spray; set aside.

2. Melt the butter in a medium saucepan over medium-low heat. Remove from the heat and stir in the brown sugar until combined. Allow the mixture to cool slightly, 5 minutes.

3. Whisk in the eggs, one at a time, followed by the vanilla, baking soda, salt, and all-purpose flour. The mixture will be thick. Fold in the cranberries, pistachios, and ½ cup of the white chocolate chips. Spread the mixture evenly into the prepared pan.

4. Bake for 22 to 26 minutes or until a toothpick inserted near the center comes out clean or with moist crumbs. Cool completely in the pan.

5. Melt the remaining white chocolate chips in a small microwaveable bowl for 15 seconds. Stir, then melt again for an additional 10 seconds until smooth. Drizzle the white chocolate evenly over the bars in the pan before cutting into squares.

Red Velvet Brownies

I used to work in a cupcake shop, and our number one best-seller was red velvet. I obviously knew about red velvet cake growing up, but I didn't realize how extremely popular this bright red flavor could be. When I started my blog, the same thing happened: people went nuts for red velvet! It made me reevaluate my life choices, and now I can say I enjoy red velvet, too. These brownies are moist, tender, and have the most delectable cream cheese icing on top! **15–18 BROWNIES**

INGREDIENTS

FOR THE BROWNIES

16 tablespoons (2 sticks) unsalted butter, cubed

2 cups brown sugar

2 large eggs

1 tablespoon vanilla extract

1 tablespoon cocoa powder

1 teaspoon baking soda

½ teaspoon kosher salt

2 cups all-purpose flour

1 ounce bottle red food coloring

FOR THE FROSTING

2 tablespoons butter, softened

4 ounces cream cheese, at room temperature

2 teaspoons vanilla extract

2 cups confectioners' sugar

1. Preheat the oven to 350°F. Line a 9-by-13 inch baking pan with foil or parchment paper, extending the sides of the foil over the edges of the pan. Spray the foil lightly with cooking spray; set aside.

2. Melt 16 tablespoons butter in a medium saucepan over low heat. Remove from the heat and cool for 5 minutes. Whisk in the brown sugar, then the eggs one at a time. Mix in 1 tablespoon vanilla extract, cocoa powder, baking soda, salt, flour, and red food coloring until combined. Pour the mixture evenly into the prepared pan.

3. Bake for 22 to 26 minutes or until a toothpick inserted near the center comes out clean or with moist crumbs. Cool completely in the pan.

4. For the frosting: Beat 2 tablespoons softened butter, cream cheese, and 2 teaspoons vanilla together with a handheld electric mixer until smooth, 1 minute. Slowly add in the confectioners' sugar, beating well until fully incorporated.

5. Spread the frosting evenly over the brownies and refrigerate for at least 1 hour to firm up the frosting before cutting into squares. Likewise, you may pipe the frosting into the brownies as shown.

Maple Gooey Butter Bars

Maple is usually a flavor everyone loves, but I don't think many consider it a holiday flavor. Why not? It's rich, comforting, cozy, and utterly delicious on a stack of pumpkin pancakes or gingerbread waffles . . . and particularly spectacular in these Maple Gooey Butter Bars! If you've never had a gooey butter cake, it's a huge deal in St. Louis. But you don't have to be from Missouri to enjoy this fantastic cross between a gooey cake and a chewy bar! **15–18 BARS**

INGREDIENTS

FOR THE CRUST

1 box yellow cake mix

8 tablespoons (1 stick) unsalted butter, melted

1 large egg

FOR THE FILLING AND TOPPING

One 8-ounce package cream cheese, at room temperature

3 large eggs

One 16-ounce box confectioners' sugar

¼ cup pure maple syrup, plus more for serving (optional)

4 tablespoons butter, melted

1 teaspoon maple extract

Additional confectioners' sugar for garnish, optional

Vanilla ice cream for serving, optional

1. Preheat the oven to 350°F. Line a 9-by-13 inch pan with foil or parchment paper, extending the sides of the foil over the edges of the pan. Spray the foil lightly with cooking spray; set aside.

2. Combine the cake mix, 8 tablespoons melted butter, and 1 egg in a large bowl until fully incorporated. Press the dough evenly in the bottom of the prepared pan.

3. For the filling: Beat the cream cheese in the bowl of a stand mixer until fluffy, 1 minute. Beat in 3 eggs, one at a time, beating well after each addition. Beat in the confectioners' sugar, followed by the maple syrup, 4 tablespoons melted butter, and maple extract. Pour the filling mixture evenly over the crust.

4. Bake for 38 to 45 minutes or until the center is just about set. If it jiggles slightly, that's okay—but you do not want to overbake it. Cool completely, then refrigerate for at least 2 hours to firm up before cutting into squares.

5. Just before serving, garnish with a sprinkling of confectioners' sugar or top with ice cream and maple syrup, if desired.

Caramel Apple Blondies

One of my favorite treats to get at fall festivals or pumpkin patches has to be a caramel apple. There's something so alluring about it, even though it's so simple. Lately people have tried to make crazy caramel apples a thing—with crushed cookies, pretzels, candy, and other ridiculous accessories—but I am an apple-simpleton and prefer mine with caramel and peanuts. These blondies have that amazing caramel apple flavor without being outrageous, which is just the way I like it! **15–18 BLONDIES**

INGREDIENTS

FOR THE BLONDIES

2 medium Granny Smith apples, peeled, cored, and roughly chopped into bite-size pieces

16 tablespoons (2 sticks) unsalted butter, plus 1 tablespoon

2 cups brown sugar

2 large eggs

1 tablespoon vanilla extract

1 teaspoon baking soda

1 teaspoon ground cinnamon

½ teaspoon kosher salt

2 cups all-purpose flour

FOR THE CARAMEL FROSTING

4 tablespoons butter, softened

¼ cup caramel sauce, plus more for garnish (optional)

¼ cup brown sugar

1 teaspoon vanilla extract

2 to 2½ cups confectioners' sugar

1. Preheat the oven to 350°F. Line a 9-by-13 inch baking pan with foil or parchment paper, extending the sides of the foil over the edges of the pan. Spray the foil lightly with cooking spray; set aside.

2. Sauté the chopped apples and 1 tablespoon of butter in a small saucepan over medium heat until softened and tender, 7 to 10 minutes. Remove from the heat and cool slightly.

3. Melt the remaining 16 tablespoons butter in a medium saucepan over medium-low heat. Remove from the heat and cool slightly, 5 minutes. Whisk in 2 cups brown sugar, then whisk in the eggs, one at a time, followed by 1 tablespoon vanilla, baking soda, cinnamon, salt, and flour. Fold in the apples. Spread the mixture evenly into the prepared pan.

4. Bake for 22 to 26 minutes or until a toothpick inserted near the center comes out clean or with moist crumbs. Cool the blondies in the pan completely.

5. For the frosting: Beat 4 tablespoons butter, caramel sauce, and ¼ cup brown sugar together in a large bowl with an electric mixer until creamy and smooth, 1 minute. Add in 1 teaspoon vanilla and 1 cup of the confectioners' sugar until well blended. Gradually add the remaining confectioners' sugar until the frosting is light and fluffy.

6. Spread the frosting evenly over the cooled blondies in the pan. Cut into squares to serve. If desired, garnish the frosted blondies with an additional drizzle of caramel sauce.

Winter Lemon Bars

Who says lemons are exclusively for spring and summer? Not I, friends. I am a lemon dessert lover year-round, and wintertime + lemon is one of my favorite combinations. When I moved to my first apartment, there was a lemon grove on the property. I'd frequently be seen with a large colander as I fished around for big, bright, juicy lemons so I could come home and make these bars. They're one of my favorites: simple, perfect, and ultra lemony! **15–18 BARS**

INGREDIENTS

FOR THE CRUST

2 cups all-purpose flour

⅓ cup granulated sugar

¼ teaspoon kosher salt

16 tablespoons (2 sticks) unsalted butter, cold and cut into cubes

FOR THE FILLING AND TOPPING

1½ cups granulated sugar

¼ cup all-purpose flour

4 large eggs

⅔ cup fresh-squeezed lemon juice

Zest of 2 lemons

Confectioners' sugar for garnish

1. Preheat the oven to 350°F. Line a 9-by-13 inch baking pan with foil or parchment paper, extending the sides of the foil over the edges of the pan. Spray the foil lightly with cooking spray.

2. For the crust: Stir together 2 cups flour, ⅓ cup granulated sugar, and salt. Using a pastry blender, cut 16 tablespoons butter into the flour mixture until the mixture resembles coarse crumbs, is slightly shaggy, and holds its shape when you grab a fistful. Press the mixture evenly into the bottom of the prepared pan and bake for 8 minutes. Remove from the oven, but keep the oven on.

3. While the crust bakes, prepare your filling: Whisk together 1½ cups granulated sugar and ¼ cup flour until fully combined. Add in the eggs, lemon juice, and lemon zest, and whisk thoroughly until the mixture is completely smooth. Pour the mixture evenly over the crust and return to the oven.

4. Bake for an additional 20 to 22 minutes or until the top is light golden brown and the center is set. If it jiggles slightly, that's okay—but you do not want to overbake. Cool in the pan completely, then refrigerate for at least 2 hours before cutting into squares. Just before serving, sprinkle the tops of the bars with confectioners' sugar.

Peanut Butter Crackle Brownies

Even though this is a holiday book focusing mainly on Christmas and Thanksgiving, I do love me some Halloween. It's so fun to dress up, but let's be real: the best part is the candy loot! Whether you're still trick-or-treating, raiding your kid's stash after their bedtime, or you have leftovers from handing it out, the candy is the best part. And one of the best candies for Halloween? Peanut butter cups, of course! These brownies have no shortage of those and pack a one-two punch of peanut butter goodness! **15–18 BROWNIES**

INGREDIENTS

1 box fudge brownie mix, plus ingredients on back of box

16 peanut butter cups, chopped

2 cups semisweet chocolate chips

1¼ cups creamy peanut butter

1 tablespoon butter

¼ teaspoon kosher salt

2 cups crispy rice cereal

1 teaspoon vanilla extract

1. Preheat the oven to 350°F. Line a 9-by-13 inch pan with foil or parchment paper, extending the sides of the foil over the edges of the pan. Spray the foil lightly with cooking spray; set aside.

2. Prepare the brownie mix according to package directions for fudge brownies. Pour the brownie mixture into the prepared pan and bake for 20 to 25 minutes or until a toothpick inserted near the center comes out clean or with moist crumbs. Remove from the oven and immediately sprinkle with the chopped peanut butter cups. Cool completely.

3. Combine the chocolate chips, peanut butter, butter, and salt in a medium saucepan over medium-low heat. Cook and stir until the mixture is smooth and melted, 5 to 7 minutes. Remove from the heat and stir in the crisp rice cereal and vanilla until fully combined. Spread the mixture evenly over the brownies.

4. Cover and refrigerate the brownies until set and firmed, at least 2 hours, before cutting into squares to serve.

Chocolate-Covered Cherry Brownie Bites

Chocolate and cherry is such a fantastic combo that I really feel needs more recognition. People go crazy over peanut butter and chocolate, and some people flip for mint and chocolate, which I totally understand. But sweet, juicy cherries and rich milk chocolate are one of the better chocolate combinations, and after trying these, I think you'll agree, too! **24 BITES**

INGREDIENTS

1 box fudge brownie mix, plus ingredients on back of box

24 chocolate-covered cherry cordials

2 squares white chocolate bark coating

Red sanding sugar sprinkles for garnish, optional

1. Preheat the oven to 350°F. Grease a 24-cavity miniature muffin pan liberally with cooking spray; set aside.

2. Prepare the brownie mix according to package directions. Scoop heaping tablespoonfuls of brownie batter evenly among the greased muffin cavities.

3. Bake for 15 to 20 minutes or until a toothpick inserted near the center of the brownie bite comes out clean or with moist crumbs. Cool for 10 minutes, then gently press a cherry cordial candy into the center of each brownie bite. Cool the brownie bites completely in the pan. Run a butter knife gently around the edge of each brownie bite to release it from the pan; place on a wire rack with parchment paper underneath.

4. Melt the white chocolate bark coating according to package directions or until smooth. Drizzle the melted white chocolate evenly over the tops of the brownie bites; immediately sprinkle with red sanding sugar, if using.

Gingerbread Blondies

I am so weird with ginger. I love ginger ale, but really dislike it in everything else. You know how certain people think cilantro tastes like soap? I feel that way about ginger—it's so strong! So when I first made these blondies, I was wary they'd be too overpowering . . . but was pleasantly surprised when I took a bite. They are perfectly spiced—just flavorful enough without feeling like you had a mouthful of soap . . . which is a good thing, since soap has no place in desserts. You're welcome in advance for this non-soapy recipe! **15–18 BLONDIES**

INGREDIENTS

FOR THE BLONDIES

16 tablespoons (2 sticks) unsalted butter

2 cups brown sugar

2 large eggs

2 teaspoons vanilla extract

1 tablespoon molasses

1 teaspoon baking soda

½ teaspoon kosher salt

1½ teaspoons ground cinnamon

¼ teaspoon ground nutmeg

⅛ teaspoon ground cloves

2 cups all-purpose flour

FOR THE FROSTING AND TOPPING

4 tablespoons unsalted butter, softened

One 8-ounce package cream cheese, at room temperature

1 teaspoon vanilla extract

2½ to 3 cups confectioners' sugar

Assorted sprinkles for decoration

1. Preheat the oven to 350°F. Line a 9-by-13 inch baking pan with foil or parchment paper, extending the sides of the foil over the edges of the pan. Spray the foil with cooking spray.

2. Melt 16 tablespoons butter in a medium saucepan over medium-low heat. Remove from the heat and whisk in the brown sugar. Let cool 5 minutes, then stir in the eggs, one at a time, followed by 2 teaspoons vanilla extract, molasses, baking soda, salt, spices, and flour, until a soft batter forms. Spread the batter evenly into the prepared baking pan.

3. Bake for 22 to 26 minutes or until a toothpick inserted near the center comes out clean or with moist crumbs. Cool completely.

4. For the frosting: Cream together 4 tablespoons butter and cream cheese in a large bowl with a handheld electric mixer until creamy and smooth, 1 minute. Beat in 1 teaspoon vanilla extract and confectioners' sugar slowly until fully incorporated and smooth.

5. Spread the frosting evenly over the cooled blondies and immediately sprinkle the top of the frosted brownies with sprinkles.

Chocolate Chip Cookie Pecan Pie Bars

My Thanksgivings are pretty low-key compared to most. For one, there are usually only eight of us at the table at any given time, and there's so much food that we all get ample leftovers. I have friends who have as much as thirty people come, and that's bananas. Can you imagine how many pies they need to bake in order to serve everyone? In that case, I always recommend these Chocolate Chip Cookie Pecan Pie Bars. They're made in a baking pan so you can cut them as large or small as you'd like . . . and everyone can get a piece, whether you're serving 8 . . . or 18! **15–18 BARS**

INGREDIENTS

One 16-ounce package refrigerated chocolate chip cookie dough, at room temperature

1 cup dark brown sugar

1 cup light corn syrup

8 tablespoons (1 stick) unsalted butter, melted

4 large eggs

1 teaspoon vanilla extract

2 cups chopped pecans

1. Preheat the oven to 350°F. Line a 9-by-13 inch baking pan with foil, extending the sides of the foil over the edges of the pan. Spray the foil liberally with cooking spray. Tear off chunks of the cookie dough and press evenly into the bottom of the pan. It may look like it won't all cover the pan, but it will!

2. Bake the cookie crust layer for 15 to 20 minutes. Remove from the oven, but keep the oven on.

3. Meanwhile, whisk together the dark brown sugar, corn syrup, melted butter, eggs, and vanilla until completely combined and brown sugar has dissolved. Fold in the chopped pecans. Pour the pecan mixture evenly over the cookie layer.

4. Return the pan to the oven and bake for an additional 25 to 30 minutes or until the center is just about set. If it jiggles slightly, that's okay—do not overbake. Cool completely, then refrigerate for 2 hours before cutting into squares.

Colorful Cookie Bars

I love a good chocolate chip cookie, but the problem is that I happen to think mine are the best! I always get a chocolate chip cookie whenever I visit a new bakery or coffee shop, and I am always underwhelmed. A perfect chocolate chip cookie, in my humble expert opinion, has to be soft and chewy with crisp outer edges and a good ratio of chips to cookie dough. And if you don't feel like rolling balls of dough, no worries—these Colorful Cookie Bars are made of my same chocolate chip cookie recipe for an easy, colorful, and most importantly—a delicious bar! **15-18 BARS**

INGREDIENTS

12 tablespoons (1½ sticks) unsalted butter, softened

1 cup brown sugar

½ cup granulated sugar

1 large egg

1 large egg yolk

1 tablespoon vanilla extract

1 teaspoon baking soda

2 teaspoons cornstarch

½ teaspoon kosher salt

2 cups all-purpose flour

¾ cup semisweet chocolate chips

¾ cup M&M's candies

NOTE: Want to make these even easier? Simply use room temperature refrigerated cookie dough and knead in the M&M's candies, or use a boxed cookie mix!

1. Preheat the oven to 350°F. Line a 9-by-13 inch baking pan with foil, extending the sides of the foil over the edges of the pan. Spray the foil with cooking spray; set aside.

2. Cream the butter, brown sugar, and granulated sugar together in the bowl of a stand mixer, beating on medium speed until creamy, 1 minute. Beat in the egg and egg yolk, followed by the vanilla extract. Beat in the baking soda, cornstarch, salt, and flour slowly until fully incorporated. Fold in the chocolate chips and M&M's candies.

3. Spread the cookie dough evenly into the prepared baking pan. Bake for 25 to 30 minutes or until the top is light golden brown and the center appears set. Cool completely before cutting into bars.

Pumpkin Churro Blondies

One of my favorite things in the world is a churro—but not all churros are created equally. For instance, churros from a certain mouse-themed theme park are the BEST, and churros from the frozen section of the grocery store tend to be lackluster. However, has anyone ever noticed that churros are always the same flavor? I'm hereby requesting all theme parks to make pumpkin churros on my behalf, because pumpkin and cinnamon sugar is a match made in culinary heaven. Mark my words! **15–18 BLONDIES**

INGREDIENTS

16 tablespoons (2 sticks) unsalted butter

2 cups brown sugar

2 large eggs

2 teaspoons vanilla extract

1 cup pumpkin puree

1 teaspoon baking soda

½ teaspoon kosher salt

2 teaspoons pumpkin pie spice

2 cups all-purpose flour

½ cup cinnamon sugar

NOTE: To make cinnamon sugar, simply mix ½ cup granulated white sugar with 2 teaspoons ground cinnamon. Don't have pumpkin pie spice? Simply use 1½ teaspoons ground cinnamon, 1 teaspoon ground ginger, ½ teaspoon ground nutmeg, and a pinch of ground cloves.

1. Preheat the oven to 350°F. Line a 9-by-13 inch baking pan with foil, extending the sides of the foil over the edges of the pan. Spray the foil lightly with cooking spray.

2. Melt the butter in a medium saucepan over medium heat. Turn off the heat and stir in the brown sugar; cool for 5 minutes.

3. Add in the eggs, one at a time, followed by the vanilla extract and pumpkin. Add in the baking soda, salt, pumpkin pie spice, and flour and stir until a soft batter comes together. Spread the batter evenly into the prepared baking pan. Immediately coat the entire surface of the blondies with the cinnamon sugar. It may seem like a lot, but a good amount will bake into the blondies, so use all of the cinnamon sugar!

4. Bake for 20 to 25 minutes or until the top is set and a toothpick inserted near the center comes out clean. Cool completely before cutting into squares.

Salted Caramel Butter Bars

My dad, Dan, is a celebrity where I live. Not only is he a very popular teacher at his high school, but he is known to bring my treats to students and faculty alike, which makes him even more beloved. While my dad is an excellent taste-tester of my goods and rarely finds something he dislikes, every time I bring over something new, he asks excitedly, "Are these salted caramel butter bars?" Most of the time, it's something new I've concocted, but sometimes I'll surprise him with his all-time favorite treat of mine. Whether you know my dad or not, you've got to try these lovable bars! **15–18 BARS**

INGREDIENTS

1 pound (4 sticks) unsalted butter, softened

1 cup granulated sugar

1½ cups confectioners' sugar

1 tablespoon vanilla extract

4 cups all-purpose flour

One 12-ounce jar caramel sauce

½ teaspoon flaky sea salt

1. Preheat the oven to 325°F. Line a 9-by-13 inch baking pan with foil or parchment paper, extending the sides of the foil over the edges of the pan. Spray the foil with cooking spray; set aside.

2. Cream the butter, granulated sugar, and confectioners' sugar together in a stand mixer over medium speed until creamy and fluffy, 3 minutes. Add in the vanilla extract and beat well. Add in the flour gradually until the dough is fully incorporated. Pat two-thirds of the dough evenly into the bottom of the prepared pan and bake for 15 minutes. Remove from the oven but keep the oven on.

3. Pour the caramel sauce evenly over the crust layer. Crumble the remaining dough evenly over the top of the caramel layer, then sprinkle the top with the sea salt.

4. Bake for an additional 25 to 35 minutes or until the top is light golden brown and the center is just about set. If the center jiggles slightly, that's okay—you do not want to overbake. Cool the bars completely, then refrigerate for at least 2 hours to firm up. Bring to room temperature for 15 minutes before cutting into squares.

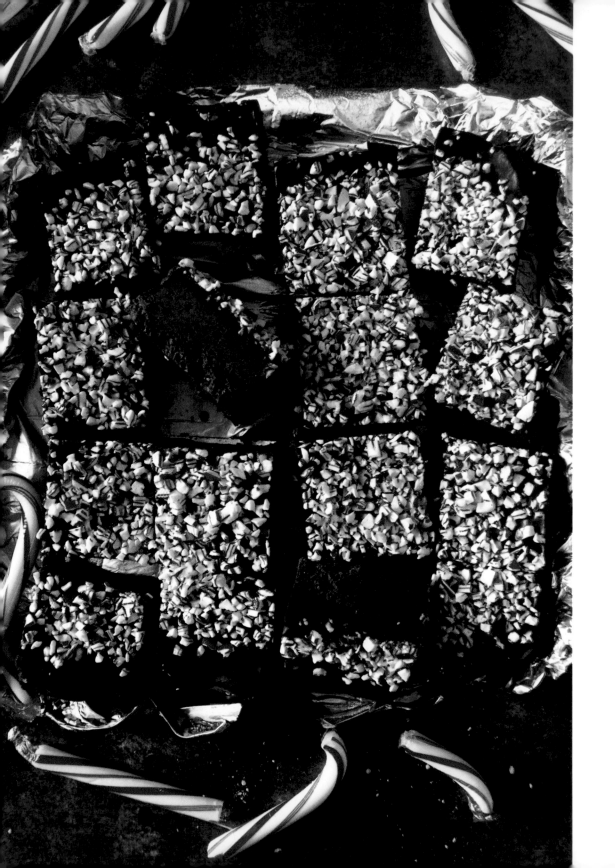

Peppermint Mocha Chewies

One of my favorite memories growing up would be waking up before the sun rose on Black Friday and heading out to Christmas shop with my mom. We'd hit up all the necessary spots to grab the must-have toys for my younger siblings, and whenever we'd pass a coffee shop, we'd pop in to order piping hot peppermint mochas. Those sweet, creamy, minty treats hit the spot and provided necessary fuel for elbowing through crazy crowds of grabby people. I should know; I'm an expert at elbowing (BTW, sorry to all those people who were elbowed by me on my caffeine-fueled shopping missions). These chewies are like little no-bake cookie bars you'll absolutely love, in a flavor I absolutely love! **12–15 BARS**

INGREDIENTS

½ cup evaporated milk

1 tablespoon espresso powder

1 cup semisweet chocolate chips, divided

½ cup finely chopped peppermint bark

One 7-ounce jar marshmallow crème

One 15.25-ounce package chocolate sandwich cookies, finely ground

1 cup confectioners' sugar

⅓ cup heavy whipping cream

⅔ cup crushed candy canes

1. Line an 8-by-8 inch baking pan with foil or parchment paper, extending the sides of the foil over the edges of the pan. Spray the foil lightly with cooking spray; set aside.

2. Combine the evaporated milk and espresso powder in a medium saucepan over medium heat, stirring until the espresso powder dissolves. Add in the chopped peppermint bark, semisweet chocolate chips, and marshmallow crème, stirring until melted and smooth. Remove from the heat.

3. Add the cookie crumbs to a large bowl. Pour the melted chocolate mixture evenly over the cookie crumbs. Stir to combine—the mixture will be thick. Spoon into the prepared pan and smooth out the top in an even layer. Cool in the fridge for 1 hour.

4. Heat the heavy whipping cream in a small bowl for 30 to 40 seconds in the microwave until hot. Add the chocolate chips to the hot cream and let sit undisturbed in the microwave for 1 minute. Stir until melted and smooth. Pour the chocolate ganache over the bars and spread in an even layer. Immediately sprinkle with the crushed candy canes. Refrigerate until firm, another hour, before cutting into bars.

Some Tips For Perfect Pies and Cheesecakes . . .

* I love baking my pie plates on top of a rimmed baking sheet in case there is any spillover from the pie. To make the mess a breeze to clean, line your rimmed baking sheet with foil beforehand!

* For recipes with a pastry crust, I highly recommend investing in a pie shield to prevent the edges of the crust from burning during the baking time. You can find pie shields at most cooking stores, some grocery stores, or even fashion your own out of strips of aluminum foil.

* In most recipes, a deep dish piecrust and plate are required due to a large quantity of filling. While grocery shopping for frozen piecrusts, look for "Deep Dish" on the package.

* In all cases, you may substitute the prepared piecrusts with your favorite homemade recipe!

4

Perfect Pies and Cheesecakes

Nothing quite says "holiday season" like pie does! These fantastic pie and cheesecake recipes are packed with flavor and personality!

Cinnamon Roll Cheesecake Pie

Cinnamon rolls have to be one of my favorite things in life. As a teen, I was a total mall-rat and would be there hanging out with different friends every weekend. My mom would give me $5 or $10 to get food, and you could bet I'd spend it all at that famous cinnamon roll place. How do people walk by and not get sucked into the intoxicating aroma of gooey, hot cinnamon rolls?! It's one of the greatest mysteries of our time. This pie is totally my homage for those many weekends eating nothing but cinnamon rolls. **8 SLICES**

INGREDIENTS

One 5-count can refrigerated cinnamon rolls

One 8-ounce package cream cheese, at room temperature

½ cup granulated sugar

1 teaspoon vanilla extract

2 tablespoons sour cream

1. Preheat the oven to 350°F. Lightly grease a 9-inch round pie pan. Open the can of cinnamon rolls and separate each roll from one another. Unroll one of the cinnamon rolls and begin to reroll it into a swirl pattern inside of the pie pan, keeping the coils loose rather than tightly swirled. Unroll another cinnamon roll and pinch the end of the first roll to the beginning of the second roll and continue to wrap the second cinnamon roll loosely around the first. Repeat with remaining rolls.

2. Combine the cream cheese, sugar, vanilla extract, and sour cream in a medium bowl and beat with an electric mixer on medium speed until combined. Fill a piping bag with the cream cheese mixture and snip off the corner of the bag. Pipe the cheesecake mixture in between the folds of the cinnamon roll swirls.

3. Bake for 20 to 30 minutes or until the top is golden brown and the center appears set. Cool for 5 minutes, then use the icing provided from the cinnamon rolls to drizzle over the top of the hot pie. Serve warm or at room temperature.

Eggnog Cream Pie

Eggnog is definitely a love-it-or-hate-it holiday item, and if you love the stuff, you'll flip for this pie! It couldn't be easier to make and only serious eggnog aficionados need apply. As for me, I usually drink one glass of eggnog during the holidays . . . but if I can drink my eggnog and eat it in a scrumptious pie, too, I'm all about that! **8–10 SLICES**

INGREDIENTS

1 small box instant vanilla pudding mix

1½ cups eggnog

½ teaspoon rum extract

½ teaspoon ground nutmeg

One 8-ounce tub whipped topping, thawed

One 9-inch round graham cracker crust

Additional whipped topping for serving, optional

1. Combine the instant pudding mix, eggnog, rum extract, and nutmeg together in a large bowl. Whisk until completely combined and mixture thickens, 2 minutes. Fold in three-quarters of the whipped topping until fully incorporated.

2. Pour the mixture evenly into the prepared piecrust and smooth out the top. Refrigerate 4 hours or until firm. Serve with remaining whipped topping, if desired.

Cranberry Marshmallow Cheesecake

I'm writing this on behalf of cranberries everywhere—cranberries are severely underrated. I love the little guys and always request them on my sandwiches, as a condiment for my Thanksgiving dinner, and as a phenomenal spread on a buttered leftover dinner roll from Christmas dinner. It's time to give cranberries the love they deserve, people! And if you love those tart, juicy berries like I do, you will definitely want to give this creamy, dreamy cheesecake a whirl. Never again will cranberries be the forgotten holiday staple! **10–12 SLICES**

INGREDIENTS

FOR THE CRUST

1 cup graham cracker crumbs

2 tablespoons brown sugar

5½ tablespoons butter, melted

FOR THE FILLING

1 envelope unflavored gelatin

Two 8-ounce packages cream cheese, at room temperature

One 7-ounce jar marshmallow crème

One 14-ounce can whole berry cranberry sauce

2 cups whipped topping, thawed

Fresh cranberries for garnish

1. Spray a 9-inch round springform pan with cooking spray. Combine the graham cracker crumbs, brown sugar, and melted butter in a medium bowl until moistened and combined. Pour the crumb mixture evenly into the prepared pan. Using your fingers or the bottom of a glass, press the crumb mixture into a crust along the bottom. Freeze until firm, 30 minutes.

2. For the filling: Sprinkle the gelatin over ¼ cup cold water in a small saucepan. Let stand for 1 minute, then heat on low until the gelatin is completely dissolved. Cool completely.

3. Beat the cream cheese and marshmallow crème in the bowl of a stand mixer until smooth and combined, 1 minute. Beat in the cranberry sauce and cooled gelatin until fully combined. Fold in the whipped topping until incorporated.

4. Pour the cheesecake mixture evenly over the piecrust. Cover and refrigerate 8 hours or overnight until completely set. Just before serving, top with fresh cranberries.

Pumpkin Cheesecake Bars

Many Thanksgivings ago when I was a wee little lass, my Grammie Pat would serve up some pumpkin pie after the main meal. I was convinced I liked pumpkin pie then, but I would find when I was given a plate, I would only eat the whipped cream and return the pie. Thankfully, my tastes have changed since then, and now pumpkin is a classic staple for me during the holiday season. However, I still need my pie slice with plenty of whipped cream! These cheesecake bars are super simple to make and are great for pleasing a crowd! **15–18 SLICES**

INGREDIENTS

FOR THE CRUST

1 box pound cake mix

2 tablespoons butter, melted

1 large egg, lightly beaten

2 teaspoons pumpkin pie spice

FOR THE FILLING

One 8-ounce package cream cheese, at room temperature

One 14-ounce can sweetened condensed milk

One 15-ounce can pumpkin puree

2 large eggs

3 teaspoons pumpkin pie spice

Fresh whipped cream for serving, optional

1. Preheat the oven to 350°F. Line a 9-by-13 inch baking pan with foil, extending the sides of the foil over the edges of the pan. Spray the foil liberally with cooking spray; set aside.

2. Combine the pound cake mix, melted butter, 1 beaten egg, and 2 teaspoons pumpkin pie spice in a medium bowl and mix until the mixture resembles wet sand and is somewhat shaggy. Pour the crust mixture evenly into the prepared pan and use your fingers to press it into an even layer. Set aside briefly.

3. For the filling: Beat the cream cheese with a handheld electric mixer in a medium bowl until fluffy, 1 minute. Add in the sweetened condensed milk, pumpkin puree, 2 eggs, and 3 teaspoons pumpkin pie spice, and continue beating on low speed until fully incorporated and totally smooth. Pour the mixture evenly over the crust in the pan.

4. Bake for 30 to 35 minutes or until the center is set and no longer jiggles. Cool completely in the pan, then refrigerate for at least 2 hours to set before serving. Just before serving, top with whipped cream, if desired.

Apple Butter Pumpkin Pie

So I know I just said pumpkin pie is a quintessential Thanksgiving staple, but can we make Apple Butter Pumpkin Pie a thing, too? I mean, trends are so easily created nowadays—in a blink, a simple pie becomes a meme and the next big thing. If you need me, I'm going to make this pie THE "it" pie of the year. By 2019, I fully anticipate it to be a full-fledged Thanksgiving phenomenon—you've heard it here first. **8–10 SLICES**

INGREDIENTS

One 9-inch deep dish frozen piecrust

1 cup apple butter

1 cup pumpkin puree

½ cup brown sugar

½ teaspoon kosher salt

1 tablespoon pumpkin pie spice

3 large eggs, slightly beaten

¾ cup evaporated milk

Fresh whipped cream for serving

1. Preheat the oven to 425°F. Place the frozen deep dish piecrust onto a rimmed baking sheet that's been lined with foil.

2. Whisk together the apple butter, pumpkin puree, brown sugar, salt, pumpkin pie spice, lightly beaten eggs, and evaporated milk in a medium bowl until completely smooth. Pour into the pie shell and gently place a pie shield around the edges of the exposed piecrust.

3. Bake for 40 to 50 minutes or until the pie is just about set. Cool completely, then refrigerate for at least 2 hours or until set before serving. Serve with whipped cream, if desired.

Maple Sugar Cream Pie

My life changed forever when I made a Sugar Cream Pie for my blog. I don't mean that facetiously—the second I posted that recipe to my website, all you-know-what broke loose. People came in droves from around the world to share their childhood memories of eating pie very similar, and my traffic quadrupled. People love their sugar cream pie! So you bet this little genius whipped up a maple version for fall. The result is every bit as good as the original, with a warming kiss of maple. And again, not joking here—it will kinda-sorta change your life forever. **8–10 SLICES**

INGREDIENTS

FOR THE PIE

One 9-inch frozen deep dish piecrust

4 tablespoons cornstarch

¾ cup granulated sugar

4 tablespoons butter, melted

2 cups heavy whipping cream

¼ cup pure maple syrup

1 teaspoon maple extract

1 teaspoon vanilla extract

FOR THE TOPPING

3 tablespoons butter, melted

⅓ cup cinnamon sugar

1. Preheat the oven to 325°F. Place the frozen deep dish piecrust onto a rimmed baking sheet that's been lined with foil. Partially bake the crust for 10 minutes. Remove from the oven, but keep the oven on.

2. While the crust bakes, whisk the cornstarch, sugar, 4 tablespoons melted butter, and heavy cream together in a medium saucepan off the heat until everything is very smooth and combined. Cook over medium heat 5 to 7 minutes, stirring constantly, until mixture is thick like pudding. Working quickly, whisk in the maple syrup and extracts and whisk until incorporated. Remove from the heat and immediately pour the filling mixture into the piecrust, smoothing out the top.

3. For the topping: Pour 3 tablespoons melted butter evenly over the pie's surface and immediately sprinkle the cinnamon sugar over the melted butter layer. It may seem like a lot of cinnamon sugar, but you want to use all of it to create that crisp crust on top.

4. Bake for 25 to 30 minutes or until the center is just about set and only jiggles a little when gently shaken. Cool completely, then refrigerate for at least 2 to 4 hours or until set and chilled.

White Chocolate Raspberry Velvet Pie

When I was flying to West Chester, Pennsylvania, to present *Two in One Desserts* on QVC, I was sitting in my airline seat reading the book, so I'd be fully prepared. Sure, even though I'd written the book and knew everything backwards and forwards, I still wanted to get to know it in its final form. The flight attendant Angel came by and asked if she could look at my book during her downtime; I agreed. Angel returned my book and found out I was headed to QVC and she immediately went on the intercom to announce to our full flight that there was a celebrity on board, and to tune in to QVC to see me and my book. I was so touched by her excitement and kindness that I connected with her after the flight. White chocolate and raspberry is her favorite combo, so this pie's for you, Angel! **8–10 SLICES**

INGREDIENTS

1½ cups white chocolate chips

⅓ cup heavy whipping cream

One 8-ounce package cream cheese, at room temperature

1 teaspoon vanilla extract

One 8-ounce tub whipped topping, thawed

One 9-inch Oreo cookie crust

⅓ cup seedless raspberry preserves

Fresh raspberries for serving

1. Microwave the white chocolate chips and heavy whipping cream together in a large bowl on high power for 30 seconds. Stir until melted and smooth; cool for 5 minutes.

2. Add the cream cheese and vanilla extract to the bowl and, using a handheld electric mixer, beat the cream cheese and white chocolate together until completely combined and smooth, 2 minutes. Fold in whipped topping until combined.

3. Pour the mixture evenly into the prepared piecrust shell and smooth out the top. There will be quite a bit of filling.

4. Microwave the raspberry preserves in a small bowl for 15 seconds or until a little softer. Spoon the raspberry preserves around the surface of the pie. Using a butter knife, swirl the cheesecake and raspberry preserves together until blended and marbled on top. Loosely cover the pie and refrigerate until firm, 4 hours. Just before serving, top with fresh raspberries.

Shortcut Pecan Pie

I'm usually not in charge of Thanksgiving dinner, but I am in charge of Christmas dinner and I need all the help I can get. Since no one in my family cooks, I'm left to my own devices to make sure I don't turn the turkey into jerky and that I use no less than 2 sticks of butter for my mashed potatoes. So when it comes to dessert, I need something foolproof that tastes amazing—not an easy feat. However, this Shortcut Pecan Pie is a winner all around for its amazing flavor and gooey texture. No one will know you took an easy way out on this pie! **8–10 SLICES**

INGREDIENTS

One 9-inch frozen deep dish piecrust

One 12-ounce jar caramel sauce, plus more for serving (optional)

3 large eggs

¼ cup brown sugar

¼ cup heavy whipping cream

1 teaspoon vanilla extract

½ teaspoon kosher salt

2 cups chopped pecans

Vanilla ice cream for serving, optional

1. Preheat the oven to 375°F. Place the piecrust on a rimmed baking sheet that's been lined with foil. Set aside.

2. Whisk together the caramel sauce, eggs, brown sugar, heavy whipping cream, vanilla extract, and salt in a medium bowl until smooth and fully combined. Stir in the chopped pecans. Pour the pecan mixture into the prepared piecrust.

3. Bake for 30 to 40 minutes or until the center is just about set and no longer jiggles when gently shaken. Cool completely, then refrigerate for at least 2 hours to set before serving.

4. Serve with ice cream and additional caramel sauce, if desired.

Chocolate Peanut Butter Pie

Is there another combination as perfect as peanut butter and chocolate? Maybe Lucy and Ricky Ricardo, but awesome as they are, they're not as delicious as the chemistry between creamy peanut butter and sweet milk chocolate. (Sorry, Ricardos.) The star of this pie is definitely the fluffy peanut butter filling with a hint of chocolate from the Oreo cookie crust and peanut butter cup topping. Of course, if you want to amp up the drama, drizzle some chocolate sauce over each slice before serving. **8–10 SLICES**

INGREDIENTS

One 9-inch Oreo cookie crust

One 8-ounce package cream cheese, at room temperature

1 cup creamy peanut butter

1 teaspoon vanilla extract

One 8-ounce tub whipped topping, thawed

1 cup peanut butter cups, roughly chopped, for serving

Additional whipped topping for serving, optional

1. Combine the cream cheese, peanut butter, and vanilla extract in a medium bowl with an electric mixer, beating until fluffy and combined, 1 minute. Fold in three-quarters of the whipped topping until fully incorporated.

2. Pour the peanut butter mixture evenly into the piecrust and smooth out the top. Refrigerate until firm, 4 to 8 hours.

3. Serve with remaining whipped topping and chopped peanut butter cups.

Frozen Rosé Pie

I have to admit: before watching *Real Housewives of Beverly Hills*, I had no idea what "rosé" even was. Pink wine seemed like something only the bourgeoisie of LA's famous zip code drank, not something peasants of Sacramento should indulge in. Oh, how I was wrong! Rosé is the bomb and I'm so glad I didn't wait until I was a 90210 resident to partake. This pie sounds crazy fancy but I promise it's totally doable and utterly divine. May I suggest making it for a midnight toast on NYE? **8–10 SLICES**

INGREDIENTS

6 ounces (¾ package) cream cheese, at room temperature

One 14-ounce can sweetened condensed milk

¾ cup rosé wine (See Note)

2 tablespoons raspberry liqueur

2 tablespoons strawberry gelatin

One 8-ounce tub whipped topping, thawed

1 deep dish graham cracker crust

Additional whipped topping and raspberries or strawberries for serving

NOTE: You may be wondering—I thought alcohol doesn't freeze? This is true, so for this recipe, look for a "low alcohol" rosé wine. I promise they're out there!

1. Beat the cream cheese in a large bowl with a handheld electric mixer until creamy, 30 seconds. Slowly beat in the sweetened condensed milk until smooth. Add in the wine, raspberry liqueur, and strawberry gelatin powder and beat on low until fully combined. Fold in the whipped topping until incorporated.

2. Pour the mixture evenly into the piecrust and smooth out the top. You may have some extra filling—spoon it into paper cups to freeze for later! Freeze the pie for at least 8 hours, preferably overnight, until frozen and firm.

3. Cut into slices and serve with additional whipped cream and assorted berries.

Apple Crisp Pie

Northern California has a hidden gem about an hour outside of Sacramento, and it's simply known as "Apple Hill." Every year, my family tries to make it up there during the crisp fall season to pick apples, get their famous pie, and try cider beer while we enjoy the gorgeous hilly views. I always take the apples I've picked to transform them into an apple pie for Thanksgiving. But you know for this book I had to sprinkle some magic fairy dust on a traditional apple pie and make it "out of the box" . . . so here we are with this Apple Crisp Pie! A fun combination between apple crisp and a classic pie, this unique version is definitely out of the box . . . and out of this world, too! 8–10 SLICES

INGREDIENTS

FOR THE PIE FILLING

5 cups Granny Smith apples, peeled, cored, and sliced

¾ cup granulated sugar

½ cup brown sugar

¼ cup cornstarch

½ teaspoon kosher salt

2 teaspoons ground cinnamon

½ teaspoon ground nutmeg

⅛ teaspoon ground cloves

One 9-inch frozen deep dish piecrust

FOR THE CRISP TOPPING

½ cup all-purpose flour

½ cup old-fashioned oats

½ cup brown sugar

½ cup granulated sugar

1 teaspoon ground cinnamon

8 tablespoons (1 stick) cold butter, cubed

1. Combine the sliced apples, ¾ cup granulated sugar, ½ cup brown sugar, cornstarch, salt, 2 teaspoons cinnamon, the nutmeg, and cloves and toss together in a large bowl. Let set for 30 minutes. While it sets, preheat the oven to 450°F. Place the frozen deep dish piecrust on a rimmed baking sheet that's been lined with foil.

2. Strain the liquid from the apple mixture and discard. Pour the apples into the piecrust—the mixture will be quite high, but remember, it will shrink down as it cooks and cools.

3. For the topping: Whisk together the flour, oats, ½ cup brown sugar, ½ cup granulated sugar, and 1 teaspoon cinnamon for the crust ingredients in a medium bowl. Use two forks or a pastry cutter to cut the cubed butter into the flour mixture until the mixture resembles coarse crumbs. Liberally top the apples with the crisp mixture. It may seem like a lot of crisp mixture, but try to pile it on!

4. Bake for 15 minutes, then reduce the oven temperature to 350°F and bake for an additional 40 to 50 minutes or until the crisp topping is golden brown and the filling is bubbly. Cool completely before cutting into slices to serve.

Oatmeal Cookie Berry Cobbler

Okay, I know cobbler is neither a cheesecake nor a pie, but this is my book and I am declaring it an integral part of this chapter! Cobbler usually evokes summertime memories for me, but why, I wonder? It's gooey, it's bubbly, it's comforting, cozy, and warm—and I am hereby changing cobbler's public persona to be a wintertime treat, too. This cobbler in particular has an oatmeal raisin cookie topping that's to die for with a piping hot mixed berry filling. If berries aren't your thing, no worries— simply sub in sliced apples, fresh cherries, or even peaches when in season. **10–12 SERVINGS**

INGREDIENTS

4 cups assorted fresh berries, halved if large (I used raspberries, blackberries, and strawberries)

¼ cup fresh lemon juice

One 16-ounce package refrigerated oatmeal raisin cookie dough

NOTE: Vanilla ice cream is almost a must for this, but I'm partial to butter pecan ice cream!

1. Preheat the oven to 375°F. Liberally grease a 9-by-13 casserole dish with cooking spray. Toss the berries with the lemon juice inside of the prepared dish and smooth into an even layer.

2. Break the refrigerated oatmeal raisin cookie dough apart with your fingers and crumble the cookie dough evenly over the berry layer. It's okay if some of the berries peek through, but try to cover everything with the cookie dough.

3. Bake for 30 to 40 minutes or until the top of the cookie is golden brown and set and the berry filling is gooey and bubbling. Cool for 15 minutes before serving.

No-Bake Peppermint Cheesecake

This may be one of my favorite recipes in this book! To me, nothing is as Christmas-y as peppermint. It evokes such a happy feeling in my soul when I step into a cozy coffee shop and I order a peppermint mocha with a candy cane swizzle stick. But if you're like me, you always want more peppermint goodness, and I'm here to deliver! This peppermint cheesecake is PACKED with peppermint flavor, so there's no missing out here! Plus, it's no-bake, which is a total lifesaver during the busyness of the holidays. Score! 10–12 SLICES

INGREDIENTS

FOR THE CRUST

25 chocolate sandwich cookies (such as Oreo), finely crushed into crumbs

4 tablespoons butter, melted

FOR THE FILLING AND TOPPING

Two 8-ounce packages cream cheese, at room temperature

1 cup confectioners' sugar

1 teaspoon vanilla extract

½ teaspoon peppermint extract

⅓ cup heavy whipping cream

1 cup peppermint baking chips

One 8-ounce tub whipped topping, thawed

Additional whipped cream and peppermint candies for garnish

NOTE: Peppermint baking chips are a seasonal item around the holidays, made by Andes brand. They're called "Peppermint Crunch Chips" and they can be found in the same section as chocolate chips. Because they're red and white, they'll turn your cheesecake pink!

1. Lightly grease a 9-inch round springform pan with cooking spray. Combine the Oreo cookie crumbs and melted butter in a medium bowl and mix until moistened. Press the cookie crumbs evenly into the bottom of the prepared pan. Freeze for 30 minutes or until firm.

2. For the filling: Beat the cream cheese and confectioners' sugar together in the bowl of a stand mixer until fluffy and smooth, 2 minutes. Beat in the vanilla and peppermint extracts. Meanwhile, combine the heavy whipping cream and peppermint baking chips in a small bowl. Microwave the peppermint chip mixture for 30 seconds, stirring until smooth and melted. Add the melted peppermint chip mixture to the cream cheese mixture and beat well to incorporate. Lastly, beat in the whipped topping until everything is combined.

3. Pour the cheesecake filling evenly into the frozen cookie crust and smooth out the top. Cover the top of the cheesecake with plastic wrap and refrigerate until set, 8 hours. Just before serving, garnish the cheesecake with additional whipped cream and peppermint candies.

Red Velvet Cheesecake

I never realized how popular red velvet was until I worked at a cupcake shop. Red velvet was easily our most popular flavor for every single holiday. One time on Christmas Eve, there was a line so long it wrapped around our building . . . all for festive red velvet cupcakes! Ever since I witnessed the mystical powers of this cake flavor, I have been trying to come up with other iterations to enjoy. This Red Velvet Cheesecake has a chewy, brownie-like texture on the bottom with a fluffy and light cheesecake on top. Easy, impressive, and you don't need to wait in line for it! **10–12 SLICES**

INGREDIENTS

FOR THE CRUST

1 box red velvet cake mix

8 tablespoons (1 stick) butter, melted

1 large egg

FOR THE FILLING

Two 8-ounce packages cream cheese, at room temperature

½ cup confectioners' sugar

1 tablespoon vanilla extract

One 8-ounce tub whipped topping, thawed

White chocolate curls for garnish, optional

1. Preheat the oven to 350°F. Lightly grease the bottom of a 9-inch round springform pan with cooking spray. Place a parchment paper round in the bottom of the pan and spray the bottom and sides of the pan once more. Set aside.

2. Combine the cake mix, melted butter, and egg in a medium bowl until thick and combined. Press the crust mixture evenly into the bottom of the prepared pan. Bake for 20 to 25 minutes or until the top is puffy and set. Cool completely.

3. For the filling: Cream together the cream cheese, confectioners' sugar, and vanilla extract in the bowl of a stand mixer until smooth, 2 minutes. Beat in the whipped topping until combined. Pour the cheesecake mixture evenly over the crust and smooth out the top.

4. Cover the cheesecake and refrigerate until set, 2 to 4 hours. Just before serving, garnish each slice with white chocolate curls, if using.

Pistachio Cream Pie

Growing up, we'd sometimes go to a spaghetti place for dinner with my grandparents. After the meal, they offered a complimentary cup of ice cream, and your choices were vanilla or spumoni. I would always go for spumoni, because three flavors are way better than one! That was my first taste of pistachio desserts, and after that memorable moment, I was hooked. This no-bake cream pie is a 50/50 cross between cheesecake and pie, but it is 100 percent delicious. **8–10 SLICES**

INGREDIENTS

1 small box instant pistachio pudding mix

1 cup milk

One 8-ounce package cream cheese, at room temperature

One 8-ounce tub whipped topping, thawed

One 9-inch prepared graham cracker crust

Additional whipped cream, chopped pistachios, and maraschino cherries for garnish

1. Whisk together the pistachio pudding mix and milk in a medium bowl until combined and thickened, 2 minutes. Add in the cream cheese and beat with an electric mixer until smooth. Fold in the whipped topping until combined.

2. Pour the mixture evenly into the prepared piecrust and smooth out the top. Cover and refrigerate for at least 4 hours or overnight before serving. Just before serving, garnish with more whipped cream, chopped pistachios, and a cherry, if desired.

5

Creative Confections

Homemade candies and miscellaneous treats are a staple for the holiday season! But before you worry about your candy-making skills, I assure you that these are super simple, totally amazing, and absolutely goof-proof. Enjoy!

Reindeer Chow

No need to worry—Reindeer Chow is just a clever name I came up with and does not involve actual food meant for reindeer. Just thought I'd clear that up before you accused me of writing a recipe for carrots intended for Santa's reindeer. Chockful of cereal, pretzels, white chocolate, M&M's and sprinkles, this mix is as addictive as it is happiness-inducing! **10 CUPS**

INGREDIENTS

7 cups rice or corn Chex cereal

2 cups miniature pretzel twists

One 11.40-ounce package peanut M&M's

One 16-ounce package white chocolate bark coating

½ cup sprinkles

1. Stir together the cereal, pretzel twists, and M&M candies in a large bowl until combined.

2. Melt the candy coating according to package directions, or until smooth. Pour the candy coating over the cereal mixture and gently toss to combine until everything is coated. Spread the mixture onto a flat, parchment paper–lined work surface in an even layer. Sprinkle liberally with the sprinkles.

3. Allow the mixture to set at room temperature for about 15 minutes before breaking into pieces and serving.

Homemade Chocolate Hazelnut Truffles

When I was growing up, we had this wonderful neighbor named Sue. Every holiday, we'd wake up and race to our mailbox because while we slept, Sue walked over and placed goodies in the mailbox for my siblings and I. In these treasured bags, we'd find erasers, pencils, and a box of chocolates, usually featuring one of these hazelnut truffles. It was so thoughtful for Sue to make our holidays a little brighter, and to this day, these chocolate hazelnut truffles continue to remind me of her kindness. **38–40 TRUFFLES**

INGREDIENTS

FOR THE TRUFFLES

3 cups finely crushed chocolate hazelnut cookies

3 cups finely chopped hazelnuts

2 cups Nutella

FOR THE COATING

Two 16-ounce packages chocolate bark coating

1 cup finely chopped hazelnuts

Star sprinkles, optional

1. Mix the crushed hazelnut cookies and 3 cups chopped hazelnuts in a large bowl until combined. Add in the chocolate hazelnut spread and stir to combine. The mixture will be thick, so you may want to use your hands. Make sure everything is moistened and coated with the chocolate hazelnut spread.

2. Line 2 cookie sheets with parchment paper. Using a cookie dough scoop, roll out tablespoon-size balls of truffles and place on the prepared baking sheets. I find it's often helpful to wet my hands with water while rolling and forming the truffles as they are quite sticky. Repeat with the remaining truffles and refrigerate or freeze until firm.

3. For the coating: Melt the chocolate bark coating according to package instructions, or until smooth. Stir in 1 cup finely chopped hazelnuts. Drop a truffle into the chocolate mixture one at a time and use a fork to coat the truffle completely with the chocolate. Use the same fork to gently lift the truffle out of the chocolate and allow the excess chocolate to drip off. Return the truffle to the baking sheet to let the chocolate set. If desired, sprinkle the set truffles with the edible star sprinkles.

Bourbon Balls

I never knew the potency of a bourbon ball until I first made them years ago for my blog. I'm not positive what I was expecting—after all, the name clearly states that they're BOURBON BALLS—but when I took a bite, I was blown away (in a good way!) by the intense bourbon flavor and awesome truffle-like texture of these potent, poppable treats. If bourbon's not your thing, substitute rum! And I think it goes without saying, but keep these bad boys away from those underage—these pack a punch! **24–26 TRUFFLES**

INGREDIENTS

One 11-ounce package vanilla wafer cookies, finely crushed

1 cup chopped walnuts or pecans

1¼ cups confectioners' sugar, divided

2 tablespoons unsweetened cocoa powder

3 tablespoons light corn syrup

1 teaspoon vanilla extract

½ cup bourbon

1. Combine the vanilla wafer crumbs, chopped walnuts, ¾ cup of confectioners' sugar, and cocoa powder in a large bowl and mix. Place the remaining confectioners' sugar in a separate small bowl.

2. Whisk together the corn syrup, vanilla extract, and bourbon in another small bowl until blended. Pour the bourbon mixture over the dry mixture and stir together until everything is moistened.

3. Roll out tablespoon-size balls of the mixture and coat the balls in the remaining confectioners' sugar. Place the coated and rolled bourbon balls onto a parchment paper–lined baking sheet to set for about 15 minutes before serving.

Chocolate Cookie Cherry Truffles

Cherries are like the holiday flavor underdog. Everyone automatically goes for gingerbread, eggnog, or peppermint, but cherries are over here like, "I'm just as worthy!" These treats consist of a chocolate–sandwich cookie truffle wrapped around a maraschino cherry, then coated in rich milk chocolate. If you want to be a little sinful, soak the cherries in vodka or rum before preparing these truffles . . . and be sure to share them with me! **18 TRUFFLES**

INGREDIENTS

16 chocolate sandwich cookies (such as Oreo)

4 ounces (½ package) cream cheese, at room temperature

18 maraschino cherries with stems, drained and patted dry

8 ounces (½ package) chocolate bark coating

Assorted sprinkles, optional

NOTE: This recipe is easily doubled or tripled depending on your needs! To make these boozy as mentioned above, simply drain the maraschino cherry liquid and replace it with vodka or rum. Let set overnight in the fridge to soak and absorb the flavor. Just before making the truffles, drain off the liquor and pat the cherries dry. Follow the recipe as stated.

1. Pulse the chocolate sandwich cookies in a food processor or blender until finely ground. Add in the cream cheese and gently combine on low speed until the cookie crumbs are moistened.

2. Line a baking sheet with parchment paper. Take a teaspoon of the cookie mixture and roll it into a ball. Press an indentation in the truffle and fill the indentation with a maraschino cherry. Gently roll the truffle mixture over and around the cherry to completely cover it, leaving the stem exposed. Place the cherry truffle onto the prepared baking sheet. Repeat with the remaining cherries, then refrigerate until firm, 20 to 30 minutes.

3. Melt the chocolate bark coating according to the package directions, or until smooth. Dip the cherry truffles into the melted chocolate, coating all parts of the truffle but leaving the stems untouched. Allow excess chocolate to drip off, then return to the baking sheet and top with sprinkles, if using. Let the chocolate coating harden before serving.

Chocolate Mint Fudge

One of my favorite things about dining out at a certain Italian restaurant is when the check comes. I know, I know—who is excited to pay at any restaurant? But at this particular place, they always include two-toned after-dinner mints with the bill, which probably softens the blow after you've ordered a few too many glasses of Moscato (I speak from personal experience). Those infamous mints are the star in this gorgeous double-decker fudge recipe! **ABOUT 50 PIECES**

INGREDIENTS

One 12-ounce package green mint chips

1 cup white chocolate chips

One 14-ounce can sweetened condensed milk

1 cup semisweet chocolate chips

⅓ cup heavy whipping cream

1 cup Andes mints, roughly chopped

1. Line an 8-by-8 square pan with foil, extending the sides of the foil over the edges of the pan. Spray the foil lightly with cooking spray; set aside.

2. Melt the green mint chips, white chocolate chips, and sweetened condensed milk together in a medium saucepan over medium-low heat, stirring constantly until smooth and melted. Remove from the heat and pour the mixture evenly into the prepared pan, smoothing out the top. Refrigerate until firm.

3. Heat the semisweet chocolate chips and heavy whipping cream together in a small microwaveable bowl for 30 seconds. Stir, then heat again for another 20 to 25 seconds until melted and smooth. Pour the chocolate mixture evenly over the mint fudge layer and smooth out the top. Immediately sprinkle on the chopped Andes mints.

4. Chill the fudge in the refrigerator for at least 2 hours or until set.

Pumpkin Spice Caramel Corn

Do you remember those popcorn tins often sold around Christmastime—
the ones with the trio of popcorn flavors inside? As a kid, I never received
them even though I lusted for them . . . but my Grammie Pat always seemed
to be gifted with them. Any time I'd come over and see a tin, my eyes would
light up as I reached for handfuls of caramel corn. I thought it was the best
thing ever . . . until I tried my caramel popcorn recipe and realized I'd been
wrong all this time! This caramel popcorn comes out perfect every time and
has a pumpkin spice twist that's irresistible! **20 CUPS**

INGREDIENTS

20 cups popped plain popcorn

16 tablespoons (2 sticks) unsalted butter

2 cups brown sugar

½ cup light corn syrup

1 teaspoon salt

1 teaspoon vanilla extract

½ teaspoon baking soda

2 teaspoons ground cinnamon

1 teaspoon ground ginger

½ teaspoon ground nutmeg

⅛ teaspoon ground cloves

1. Preheat the oven to 200°F. Pour the popcorn
evenly among two large roasting pans.

2. Melt the butter, brown sugar, corn syrup, and salt
together in a medium saucepan over medium heat.
Bring the mixture to a boil and boil for 5 minutes,
stirring constantly. Remove from the heat and
whisk in the vanilla extract, baking soda, and
spices.

3. Pour the hot caramel mixture evenly over the
popcorn in the pans. Note that the caramel will
not coat all of the popcorn immediately, but as you
bake it, the caramel will thin out enough to coat it
completely.

4. Bake for 1 hour, stirring once every 15 minutes to
coat the popcorn entirely with the caramel mixture.
Cool in the pans completely before breaking into
pieces to serve.

Salted Nut Roll Truffles

When I was growing up, there was a period of time when my dad was a stay-at-home dad. I thought it was awesome: we woke up and watched *The Price is Right* together and for lunch he'd frequently make me fluffernutter sandwiches. If you've never heard of a fluffernutter, it's the glorious thing that happens when you combine marshmallow and peanut butter. Hey, don't knock it until you try it—preferably in these spectacular truffles! **36–38 TRUFFLES**

INGREDIENTS

½ cup creamy peanut butter

½ cup honey

1 cup nonfat dry milk powder

½ teaspoon vanilla extract

36 miniature marshmallows

1 cup finely chopped peanuts

1. Line a baking sheet with parchment paper or a silicone liner; set aside.

2. Mix the peanut butter, honey, dry milk powder, and vanilla extract with a handheld electric mixer in a medium bowl for 1 to 2 minutes, or until combined. Roll out a teaspoon-size ball of dough and flatten it in your hand. Place a miniature marshmallow in the center of the dough, then roll the dough around the marshmallow to cover it completely. Repeat with remaining truffles.

3. Dredge the truffles into the finely chopped peanuts to coat, then let set on the prepared pan for 20 minutes before serving.

Pecan Praline Bark

One of my fondest high school memories doesn't even involve school—it involves dating a boy, going to his house all the time, and his mom making this bark. Hi, Stacy! I fondly remember her son and I coming home from the movies or the mall and smelling the luscious aroma of butter and brown sugar bubbling on the stove. I watched with glee as Stacy poured the boiling mixture over graham crackers and pecans and baked it until it was perfectly golden. The hardest part was definitely waiting for the molten candy to cool before we could break it into pieces and nosh on it the whole day! **8 SERVINGS**

INGREDIENTS

2 sleeves honey graham crackers

16 tablespoons (2 sticks) salted butter

1 cup brown sugar

1 teaspoon vanilla extract

1½ cups chopped pecans

½ cup white chocolate chips, melted (optional)

1. Preheat the oven to 400°F. Line a rimmed baking sheet with parchment paper or foil, taking care to cover the edges of the pan. Spray the pan lightly with cooking spray. Arrange the graham crackers evenly all over the bottom of the pan, breaking some graham crackers to fit into smaller cracks; set aside.

2. Combine the butter and brown sugar in a medium saucepan and bring to a boil over medium heat. Boil for 2 minutes exactly, stirring constantly. Remove from the heat and stir in the vanilla extract and chopped pecans.

3. Pour the hot mixture evenly over the graham crackers, trying your best to coat all of the crackers. Bake for 7 minutes, then remove from the oven and cool completely before breaking into squares. Drizzle with melted white chocolate, if using.

Chocolate Hazelnut Fudge

Remember when I said I ate a lot of junk food growing up? Well, it's true—and it took one fateful day in French class my sophomore year to learn about Nutella, a.k.a. Heaven. Our French teacher had promised us homemade crepes with Nutella filling and once I took a bite of that hot crepe stuffed with gooey Nutella, I was sold and began asking for it every time my mom would grocery shop. What's not to love? That same gooey texture we know and love is in this fudge—also known as Heaven. **50 PIECES**

INGREDIENTS

One 14-ounce can sweetened condensed milk

1 package bittersweet chocolate chips

½ cup Nutella

1 teaspoon vanilla extract

1 cup chopped hazelnuts

1. Line an 8-by-8 inch square pan with foil, extending the sides of the foil over the edges of the pan. Spray the foil lightly with cooking spray; set aside.

2. Melt the condensed milk, bittersweet chocolate chips, and Nutella together in a medium saucepan over medium-low heat, stirring constantly until smooth. Remove from the heat and stir in the vanilla extract and chopped hazelnuts.

3. Spread the fudge mixture evenly into the prepared pan and smooth out the top. Refrigerate covered for 4 hours or until set.

Christmas Crack

Toffee used to be on my List of Things Hayley Fears. Why, you ask? Because molten sugar is scary, and candy thermometers are even scarier! Well, turns out, neither of these things are actually that frightening as I'd mentally hyped them out to be. This Christmas Crack recipe is so easy; you don't even need a candy thermometer—just a simple timer. It's so easy, even the 'fraidy cats among us can do it! **8 CUPS**

INGREDIENTS

45 to 50 butter club crackers

16 tablespoons (2 sticks) salted butter

1 cup light brown sugar

1 teaspoon vanilla extract

1 package semisweet chocolate chips

1½ cups miniature M&M's candies

½ cup sprinkles

NOTE: This toffee recipe is super versatile! Experiment with graham crackers or saltine crackers instead of the butter club, and try different candies sprinkled on top after baking. This would be particularly delicious with chopped peanut butter cups, broken up Butterfinger candies, or even crushed candy canes!

1. Preheat the oven to 400°F.

2. Line a rimmed 10-by-15 inch baking sheet with foil or parchment paper. Grease the foil lightly with cooking spray. Arrange the crackers evenly on the prepared pan, fitting them side-by-side so they cover the bottom completely. Break the crackers if necessary to fit into cracks. Set aside.

3. Combine the butter, brown sugar, and vanilla extract in a medium saucepan. Bring to a boil over medium heat, stirring constantly for 3 minutes. Remove from the heat and pour the toffee mixture evenly over the crackers in the pan. It's okay if the toffee mixture doesn't coat every cracker as it will spread some while it bakes.

4. Bake for 7 minutes. Remove from the oven and immediately add the chocolate chips evenly over the top of the hot toffee. Let set for about 5 minutes, and then use an offset spatula to spread the chocolate evenly over the toffee. Immediately top the melted chocolate with the miniature M&M's candies and sprinkles. Allow to cool completely and set before breaking into squares.

Sugar Cookie Truffles

The idea for these truffles came to me long, long ago—back when I first started my blog, in 2011! I was in the dollar store, one of my favorite places, and spotted some cookie truffles in the seasonal aisle. I was perplexed—what in the world was a cookie truffle?! Inspired, I bought them and was crestfallen when they weren't that good (why do you toy with my emotions, dollar store candy!). However, I knew I had to make my own, and I've been making versions of these ever since. You won't believe how easy and tasty these are! **14–15 TRUFFLES**

INGREDIENTS

18 to 20 hard sugar cookies

4 ounces (½ package) cream cheese, softened

1 teaspoon vanilla extract

8 ounces (½ package) white chocolate bark coating

Sprinkles

NOTE: For a festive touch, try adding small jimmies to the cookie truffle dough before rolling into truffles. Each bite will be packed with a sprinkly surprise! About a quarter cup of sprinkles should be perfect.

1. Pulse the sugar cookies in a food processor until they become fine crumbs. Add in the cream cheese and vanilla extract and pulse on low speed until fully incorporated and the mixture is combined. Line a baking sheet with foil or parchment paper.

2. Use a small teaspoon to scoop balls of dough from the food processor. Roll the dough balls in your hand and place them on the prepared baking sheet. Repeat with the remaining dough balls.

3. Freeze the dough balls until firm, 20 minutes. Melt the white chocolate bark coating according to package directions, or until smooth.

4. Use a fork to dunk each truffle one at a time into the melted candy coating. Coat all sides of the truffle with the melted white chocolate, then use the fork to gently lift the truffle and tap off the excess chocolate. Return the coated truffle to the baking sheet and immediately top with sprinkles. Repeat with the remaining truffles. Allow the truffles to set completely before serving.

Peanut Butter Buckeye Pretzels

Now most people know I'm not the biggest chocolate and peanut butter fan. It's probably a birth defect of some kind, to be honest, but I've learned to live with my differences. It's called perseverance, people! However, I aim to please and I know most folks can't get enough of creamy peanut butter and smooth milk chocolate . . . so here I am with these delightful Buckeye Pretzels. And full confession: I adore these! Perfectly petite, irresistible, slightly addictive sweet-and-salty goodness in every bite! **60 PRETZEL BITES**

INGREDIENTS

¾ cup creamy peanut butter

4 tablespoons cup unsalted butter, softened

½ teaspoon vanilla extract

1½ cups confectioners' sugar

120 miniature pretzel twists

One 16-ounce package chocolate bark coating

Sprinkles, optional

1. Line a rimmed baking sheet with foil or parchment paper and set aside.

2. Combine the peanut butter, softened butter, and vanilla extract in a large bowl and beat well with an electric mixer until smooth, 2 minutes. Gradually add in the confectioners' sugar, beating well on low speed until fully incorporated. The mixture should look a little shaggy but hold its shape when pinched between your fingers.

3. Use a teaspoon-size cookie dough scoop to create little round balls of dough. Press the dough ball in between two pretzel twists, pushing slightly to create a mini pretzel sandwich. Repeat with the remaining truffle dough and remaining pretzels; place them all on the prepared baking sheet and refrigerate for at least 1 hour to firm up.

4. Melt the chocolate bark coating according to package directions, or until smooth. Working one at a time, dunk half of the pretzel bite into the chocolate and allow excess chocolate to drip off. Return to the baking sheet and sprinkle the chocolate-coated side of the truffle with sprinkles, if using. Repeat with the remaining truffles. Allow the chocolate to set before serving.

Polar Bear Paws

INGREDIENTS

One 11-ounce package caramels, unwrapped

3 tablespoons heavy whipping cream

1 tablespoon unsalted butter

1 teaspoon vanilla extract

1¼ cups unsalted dry-roasted peanuts

One 16-ounce package white chocolate bark coating

NOTE: I'm not kidding with you—please let the candies come to room temperature before serving! Your teeth will lose a battle with cold caramel, so consider yourself warned!

1. Line a rimmed baking sheet with foil or parchment paper, and lightly grease it with cooking spray.

2. Combine the caramels, heavy whipping cream, and butter in a medium microwaveable bowl. Microwave on high power for 90 seconds, stopping to stir the mixture every 30 seconds. It may be hard to stir around the 30- and 60-second mark, but try your best. Around the 90-second mark, it should be smooth and glossy. Whisk in the vanilla extract and peanuts and stir to combine.

3. Allow the mixture to rest for about 10 minutes, which will give the caramels a chance to firm up a bit. Using a buttered spoon, drop heaping tablespoonfuls of the hot caramel mixture onto the prepared baking sheet. The size of your spoon determines how many candies you should get out of this mixture.

4. Freeze the caramel mounds until firm and completely solid, 30 to 45 minutes. After freezing, melt your white chocolate bark coating according to package directions, or until smooth.

5. Use a fork to dunk the caramel mounds into the white chocolate bark coating, making sure to coat all sides. Remove the coated caramel mound carefully, allowing excess white chocolate to drip off. Return to the baking sheet and repeat with the remaining caramels. Allow the coated candies to come to room temperature completely before serving.

As a teen, my best friend, Katrina, and I would go to this local run-down mall. Back then it was a lame mall, and today it's still a lame mall, but they had our teenage essentials: punk rock store, orange smoothie place, cheap movie theater, and See's Candies. Katrina and I would do a few laps around the mall, talk to the cutie who worked at the punk store, grab an orange smoothie to split and get a major sugar high, go see a $2 movie, and then crawl to See's Candies to grab a coveted Polar Bear Paw. These "paws" are actually gooey caramel mixed with peanuts and coated in white chocolate . . . and they are beyond easy to make! Teenage Hayley is totally high-fiving current Hayley right now . . . wait, do people still high-five? **18–20 CANDIES**

Southern Pralines

I am not southern at all (California girl born and raised), but I'd like to adopt some of the southern traditions—namely, southern food. Jambalaya, gumbo, beignets, fried chicken—I love it all, but my top favorite southern treat has to be pralines! Californians seriously don't know what they're missing, because pralines are the bomb diggity! Like a cross between a tender cookie and a melt-in-your-mouth candy, these buttery brown sugar treats are studded with pecans and are super addictive. Bet you can't have just one! **20–24 CANDIES**

INGREDIENTS

1½ cups chopped pecans

1½ cups granulated sugar

¾ cup brown sugar

4 tablespoons plus 2 tablespoons unsalted butter, cubed

½ cup evaporated milk

1 teaspoon vanilla extract

½ teaspoon kosher salt

1. Line two muffin tins with 20 to 24 paper liners; set aside. Meanwhile, combine the chopped pecans, granulated sugar, brown sugar, butter, evaporated milk, vanilla extract, and salt in a medium saucepan over medium-high heat.

2. Bring the mixture to a boil, stirring constantly until a candy thermometer reads between 235°F and 240°F, around 10 minutes. Remove the pan from the heat and working quickly and carefully, beat the mixture vigorously with a wooden spoon until the candy becomes opaque and thick, 3 to 5 minutes.

3. After the mixture thickens, use a cookie dough scoop to portion the candy evenly among the prepared muffin tins—about one scoop per muffin cavity. Allow the candy to set completely before peeling back the muffin liners to serve.

Christmas Cracker Stackers

When I was a kid, I loved making Christmastime treats. Usually this meant decorating sugar cookies from the store using canned frosting and hundreds of colorful sprinkle options (when I wasn't pouring the sprinkles directly into my mouth like the sugar addict I am). Little did I know there were infinite possibilities for Christmasy treats, including these Christmas Cracker Stackers. What is a cracker stacker? It's basically a sweet and salty flavor bomb nestled between two buttery round crackers, then coated in chocolate. Enlist the kids to help add a festive touch with sprinkles on top! **48 PIECES**

INGREDIENTS

96 butter round crackers (such as Ritz)

1½ cups marshmallow crème

1½ cups creamy peanut butter

Two 16-ounce packages chocolate bark coating

Assorted sprinkles for garnish, optional but recommended

NOTE: Don't like marshmallow crème? Substitute the marshmallow for cookie butter spread or even chocolate hazelnut spread!

1. Line two rimmed baking sheets with foil or parchment paper and set aside.

2. Spread half of the butter crackers with the marshmallow crème. Spread the remaining butter crackers with the peanut butter. Sandwich the two crackers together to create a cracker stacker. Place the cracker stackers on the prepared baking sheets and refrigerate until firm, 20 to 30 minutes.

3. Melt the chocolate bark coating according to package directions, or until smooth. Dunk each cracker stacker one at a time into the candy coating, allowing excess chocolate to drip off. Return to the baking sheets and immediately sprinkle the tops with sprinkles, if using. Repeat with the remaining cracker stackers and allow treats to set completely before serving.

Acknowledgments

Writing a cookbook is not easy, and I have a lot of people to thank for my third book-baby!

To my mom and my dad, who are always game to taste-test anything and everything, even if it's normally a flavor you'd avoid like the plague. Thank you for supporting my dr eams and supporting me as a human while I job-hopped and cried until I finally found an unconventional career that I love.

To my brother, Alex, and my sister, Chloe—thank you for your loyalty and support throughout the writing process and always. Thanks for offering your keen eyes for detail in helping me stage the perfect shot with the best props.

To my puppies, Mannie and Jack, for always making me smile and keeping my kitchen floor—littered with rogue sprinkles—clean.

To my family and friends, all of whom were ready and willing to be guinea pigs for my insane creations both for this book and otherwise. Thanks for always making me laugh with a ridiculous meme or funny story, for bringing me wine at the end of a long day baking, and for supporting me even though I was MIA while writing this book.

A super-huge thank-you to my super-woman lawyer Sara Hawkins for always being in my corner. You make my world every time you say "congratulations! You're writing another cookbook!"

Major thanks to the wizards of Countryman Press including but not limited to Ann Treistman, Aurora Bell, Devorah Backman, and Becca Kaplan for putting up with me and my craziness and for asking me to write not one, not two, but THREE cookbooks! I am so grateful for all your hard work, knowledge, and support.

And a huge, massive, enormous THANK YOU to all of the readers of my books and of my blog, *The Domestic Rebel*. Your support, loyalty, and encouragement are so invaluable to me and motivates me to think "out of the box" to create amazing recipes and hilarious stories for you to share and enjoy. Thanks for subscribing to my blog; for pinning my recipes all over Pinterest; for your likes, comments, and shares on my social channels; and for buying my books and rooting me on! YOU are the reason I continue to push myself to be the best blogger and author I can be, so THANK YOU.

XOXO, Hayley

Index